D1067722

The Unmuzzled MAX

The Unmuzzled MAX

by Max Ferguson

With a foreword by Allan McFee

Illustrated by Roy Condy

McGraw-Hill Ryerson Limited

Toronto   Montreal   New York   London   Sydney
Johannesburg   Mexico   Panama   Düsseldorf
Singapore   Rio de Janeiro   Kuala Lumpur   New Delhi

THE UNMUZZLED MAX

ISBN 0-07-092989-0

1 2 3 4 5 6 7 8 9 D71 0 9 8 7 6 5 4 3 2 1

Printed and Bound in Canada

FOREWORD

You get up in the morning and often wonder or, indeed, say to yourself, "Will I be able to do it again today, the old grind, the same old routine?" We all feel this way sometimes, and when we do, it is perhaps the very familiarity of "the same old routine" that gets us through. Now look with me, if you will, at Max Ferguson as I have seen him day after day for something like seven years, sitting in the predawn silence of the old CBC building on Jarvis Street in cindery downtown Toronto. No old grind or same old routine here to pull on like a familiar hair shirt, however uncomfortable.

No. This was a time, as expected by millions of devoted listeners, for creativity, a time to come up with something new and different, something clever gleaned from the morning newspaper. But it must have been a time of complete loneliness too, as the on-air deadline got closer and closer.

5:30 A.M. and Max is starting to glance through the morning paper.

6:00 A.M. . . . . "Doesn't seem to be much in the news today." . . . Dig a little deeper . . . something's bound to occur, some interest besides the birth columns and want-ads. Whatever became of those last 30 minutes?

6:30 A.M. . . . . Good God, nothing's happened in the way of an idea. The birth announcements and the want-ads are still there; add to these the death column . . . Can't think about that . . . it hits too close to home at this point.

The sound effects man is quietly waiting for instructions, the operator the same, the producer as well, all waiting to relay the result of Max's birth pangs which are due to go on the air to an entire country just one hour from now (7:35 A.M. to the Maritimes, taped at that time and relayed across the nation to be presented at the appropriate time in each time zone).

When I arrived at 6:45 A.M. as your affable friendly announcer, one glance at Max would tell me how the "skits" were coming. On a very good skit day he would be sitting back in relaxed fashion with very little throat clearing going on. The sound effects man would be digging up sounds in another part of the building, the operator contentedly reading the paper, the producer's face wreathed in smiles. Two skits ready to go on the air.

> God's in His Heaven,
> All's right with the world.

On a just plain good day, instructions on one skit issued, tension in the air, working on the second skit, a great deal of throat clearing, rather glassy-eyed and mildly hysterical sound effects man searching for sound effects, operator not reading the paper now but staring straight ahead waiting, producer staring at the same spot, waiting; Max's throat clearing reaching crescendo proportions.

> Down the long and silent street,
> The dawn, with silver-sandaled feet,
> Crept like a frightened girl.

On a really bad day, not sure of either skit: sound effects man staring straight ahead and waiting, operator eyes closed and waiting, producer with filmed eyes, waiting, Max's throat clearing like a Gatling Gun. On mornings such as this my cheery and ringing "Good-morning" was left hanging like limp spaghetti on the hand of rosy-fingered dawn.

In my early days with the program, I wondered many times if it would even get on the air. But always, unfalteringly excellent, the program went on the air and Max Ferguson's name became a household word across Canada and his skits a morning addiction for many millions of Canadians.

In spite of my close association with Max over those years, I always wondered how he did it day after day. Now, for the first time, the secret is revealed in the pages that follow, a collection of what he considered to be his best skits. I've read them and I recommend them highly to you. If you are a true Max Ferguson fan, most (and perhaps all) of them will come back to you as they did to me with nostalgic delight. For the past few years there have been many books published dealing with the secret of instant success in a multitude of fields. This may be one of them and may serve to make *you* an instant success in broadcasting, a master of biting satire, the breakfast toast of a nation.

Mind you, I don't guarantee it, but it's all here before you.

vi

All you need is a handy scrap of paper (the flap of a cigarette box would do) and the mind of a Max Ferguson. Nothing to it.

Toronto,   Allan McFee
October, 1971.

THE GREAT TORY METAPHOR

The big political story of 1966 was the November Tory leadership conference called by the Dalton Camp faction to review the past record of John Diefenbaker. Dief strongly objected, arguing that you can't have a leadership convention when the leadership isn't vacant. One of his aides told the press: "It's like a marriage ceremony . . . you can't have a wedding if one of the partners is already married!"

THE SCENE:

An excited gathering of Tories, in a Convention Hall of the Chateau Laurier in Ottawa, await the crucial speeches of the two protagonists . . . Diefenbaker and Camp.

AIDE *(Raising his voice over the din and the music)*: Well, Chief, there's no sign of Dalton Camp yet.

DIEFENBAKER: Uh . . . he'll be along all right. Rest assured of that! Hmmmm . . . a splendid turnout!

AIDE: Yes, this confrontation between you and Mr. Camp certainly has created a lot of interest!

DIEFENBAKER: Uh . . . I understand that I'll be speaking first . . . uh, before Camp.

AIDE: That's correct sir. I guess you have your speech all ready?

DIEFENBAKER: Uh, yes indeed. As a matter of fact, I plan to rely heavily on that extremely felicitous metaphor of yours . . . uh, the one you gave out to the press.

AIDE: Oh! Well, I'm pleased you liked it . . . very flattered, sir!

DIEFENBAKER: Yes, I thought it was a masterpiece . . . a fine stroke . . . uh . . . a veritable tour de force . . . uh . . . how does it go, again?

AIDE: Well, I simply compared this whole question of a leadership conference to a marriage ceremony ... you can't have a wedding if one of the partners is already married!

DIEFENBAKER: Ah, yes! That's it. I like that! My entire speech will be built around that premise. You know, all through this bitter wrangling, our opponents . . . the forces of Dalton Camp . . . have relied on prosaic, unimaginative, pedestrian prose. Well, that may be all right for the mind. Uh, but one should never forget the heart. Over the many years that I've spent in the political arena, I've learned that you can't beat the sentimental appeal . . . poetry, imagery, metaphors, similes, allegory. . . . These are the persuasive weapons that enable one to fight one's way straight into the hearts of an audience.

AIDE: I agree. . . . I think this idea of yours will go over.

DIEFENBAKER: Uh . . . there's no doubt about it. That metaphor about the marriage ceremony . . . that's the kind of literary technique that strikes home.

AIDE: I'm surprised our opponents haven't tried to pick that metaphor up and twist it to their advantage.

DIEFENBAKER: Uh . . . not likely . . . no imagination . . . no sensibility . . . hard-hitting facts are all they're after. No, this little metaphor is all our own and when I get up there on the platform, mark my words, I'll use it to advantage!

AIDE: Excuse me, sir! Look over there! Looks like the Camp crowd coming into the hall now. Yes! There's Dalton Camp ... I can just ... Oh!

DIEFENBAKER: Eh? What is it?

AIDE: Oh ... no! Surely he wouldn't dare!

[*The swelling strains of the Lohengrin Wedding March fill the hall.*]

DIEFENBAKER: Uh . . . the scoundrel! He's stolen our metaphor! Uh . . . Just look at that . . . the whole works . . . the white veil . . . carrying red roses . . . five flower girls behind him . . . wouldn't you know! You played right into his hands!

AIDE: But, sir ... I ... I ...

DIEFENBAKER: Why did you have to come up with that stupid metaphor in the first place?

2

AIDE: But ... but ... sir! I thought you liked it.

DIEFENBAKER: Uh ... you couldn't stick to plain, hard-hitting everyday language, could you? Oh no! You had to use a metaphor!

AIDE *(Crushed)*: I ... I ... I'm sorry sir.

DIEFENBAKER *(Stomping off)*: If there's anything I hate ... after Dalton Camp ... it's a metaphor!!!!

A COMPUTER ALWAYS DOES ITS BEST

In May, 1967, thirteen hundred Canadian and American Boy Scouts took part in a huge Camporee in Philadelphia. For the first time, a computer was used to ensure compatibility in the pairing off of tent-mates. It did such a great job that even torrential rains, which washed out the entire camp, couldn't dampen the high morale. One drenched lad, it was reported, stood beaming in the mud of the evacuated camp and told his Scouter: "Gee, this is the best camp I've ever been to!"

THE SCENE:

In a sea of mud, lashed by wind and rain, sits the little headquarters hut of Scouter Al and Scouter Bob. Inside, plans are laid for the evacuation.

SCOUTER AL: Scouter Bob?

SCOUTER BOB: Yes, Scouter Al?

SCOUTER AL: Is all the equipment loaded on the buses?

SCOUTER BOB: Yeah ... all ready to go.

SCOUTER AL: And the tents? Are they all packed?

SCOUTER BOB: Just about. I think there's only one more to come down . . . young Waldo's on the far side of the camp.

SCOUTER AL: Still holding out, eh? What a plucky little kid!

SCOUTER BOB: Yeah. I went by there about ten times this morning. Kept yelling to evacuate each time but he kept yelling back that he wanted to see it through right to the end.

SCOUTER AL: Bless his little heart!

SCOUTER BOB: Yeah . . . sort of epitomizes the whole scouting movement.

[*A knock is heard on the hut door.*]

SCOUTER AL: Yes? Come in?

WALDO (*A bit adenoidal*): Hi, Scouter Al . . . Scouter Bob!

BOTH: How are you, Waldo!

WALDO: Golly, I know I've been in here a few times already, but I just wanted to tell you again . . . this is the best darn camp I've ever been to. . . . I really mean it!

[*Door slams and he's gone.*]

SCOUTER AL: Great little guy. No storm's gonna dampen that kind of morale!

SCOUTER BOB: You know, Scouter Al, this would make a great piece of public relations.

SCOUTER AL: One jump ahead of you, Scouter Bob! I've already arranged for some coverage. The reporters are on their way right now to do a story on that little trouper!

SCOUTER BOB: Great! Boy, I really don't know how he stays out in that kind of weather. I know I couldn't have done it at his age.

SCOUTER AL: Well, I think we've gotta give a bit of credit to that computer. I mean no matter how plucky the kid was, he wouldn't survive this downpour holed up in a pup tent with some kid he couldn't stand.

SCOUTER BOB: Oh, no doubt about that. The computer's done a bang-up job. I was just glancing through some of these cards . . . these kids have been paired off like peas in a pod. Well, I mean, you take young Waldo and his tent buddy . . . look at this . . . they're the same age to the month. . . .

SCOUTER AL: Great.

SCOUTER BOB: Same religion.

SCOUTER AL: That sure helps!

SCOUTER BOB: And get this . . . their fathers are both doctors!

SCOUTER AL: How about that!

SCOUTER BOB: Same academic standing at school . . . it just goes on and on . . . same hobbies . . . collecting stamps and birds' eggs . . . one likes to sell apples from door to door and sure enough, the other also likes to sell. . . . Oh my God! . . . Oh, no! . . . I never even noticed this! . . . the other likes to sell cookies!!!

[*Another knock is heard on the hut door.*]

SCOUTER AL: Come in?

WALDO: Hi, Scouter Al . . . Scouter Bob! I hope I'm not a nuisance but, wow, I've just gotta tell the whole world about this camp, I really. . . .

SCOUTER BOB: Come here, you!

WALDO: Pardon?

SCOUTER AL: You rotten little kid!!!

WALDO: What's wrong, Scouter Al?

SCOUTER AL: Don't play the wide-eyed innocent with me, Rasputin! I'll give you two minutes to get that girl guide out of that pup tent and get onto that bus with the rest of the boys!

WALDO: Aw, gee, Scouter Al. . . .

SCOUTER BOB: *(Shoving him out the door)*: Get out of here. God help you if Baden Powell ever hears about this! *(The door slams.)* Gee . . . what an ornery, rotten kid!

SCOUTER AL: Scouter Bob . . . I've been in scouting most of my life working with boys. Somehow, I just can't bring myself to call him "a rotten kid." There's just got to be a reason for what he did!

SCOUTER BOB: What do you mean, Scouter Al? No young scout behaves like that!

SCOUTER AL: That's just the point, Scouter Bob, I think we were both hoodwinked. Waldo's *got* to be . . . a dwarf!

THOU SHALL NOT

I don't suppose many Canadians, outside of Toronto, have ever heard of Etobicoke and yet this borough, part of Metropolitan Toronto, it quite unique. Not just because it refuses to sound the final two letters of its name but because it seems to live in a little world of its own with, I'm sure, the world's largest collection of restrictive by-laws. Kids can't build treehouses, kittens must be on a leash in public and piano lessons can not be given in private homes. The last I heard, they were making it illegal to blow any horn or ring any bell or cause anything to be blown or rung which might disturb the residents.

THE SCENE:

Two elderly ladies, red-eyed and clutching moist lace hankies, stand outside a quiet Etobicoke church. The soft, sad strains of organ music drift out to mingle with the hushed tones of the small, sombre crowd standing on the sidewalk.

FIRST LADY: That was a lovely service . . . so deeply moving.

SECOND LADY: Oh, yes. I thought the minister said just the right things.

FIRST LADY: So often, you know, on occasions such as this the minister can overdo things and it all becomes so mawkish and embarrassing.

SECOND LADY: You know, I felt the parents held up so magnificently.

FIRST LADY: Oh, yes. It . . . it was their only daughter I understand.

SECOND LADY: Yes . . . *(A dainty nose blow)* . . . their only daughter.

FIRST LADY: That always makes it so much more difficult.

6

SECOND LADY: Indeed it does.

SANCTIMONIOUS VOICE: Excuse me, ladies, but are you members of the immediate family?

SECOND LADY: No, no we're not. Just very old friends of the family.

SANCTIMONIOUS: I see. Well, the limousines will be moving off in a moment. Perhaps you'd both like to ride in this one over here.

FIRST LADY: Thank you very much.

SANCTIMONIOUS: I'll just open the door for you.

[*Car door opens . . . closes. Car moves off.*]

FIRST LADY: Wasn't it wonderful, too, the way the children behaved.

SECOND LADY: Yes, there's nothing worse at a time like that than to have children acting up . . . laughing thoughtlessly . . . running around.

FIRST LADY: Yes, even though they were quite young they seemed to sense the dignity of the occasion.

SECOND LADY: Such a tribute to the parents.

FIRST LADY: And those folk standing around outside after the service. I knew just how they felt . . . wanting to say something and yet not quite knowing what to say.

SECOND LADY: Well they did the best thing . . . just stood there as a mark of quiet respect.

FIRST LADY: You know, Pauline, I've been through this sort of thing in cities all across Canada but it's never quite like this.

SECOND LADY: Yes. No matter where you go . . . for quiet dignity you just can't beat an Etobicoke wedding.

CHAUFFEUR: Hey, you know? I thought they made a pretty good lookin' couple!

FIRST LADY: What!

SECOND LADY (*With equal horror*): What did you say, young man?

CHAUFFEUR: I said I thought they made a pretty good lookin' couple.

FIRST LADY: There's certainly no need to be bawdy, driver!

CHAUFFEUR: Gee . . . I'm sorry . . . I didn't mean to. . . .

7

SECOND LADY: And will you stop shouting! You're not in downtown Toronto now. You're in Etobicoke!!!

LEAVING IT ALL BEHIND

Shortly after Lester Pearson vacated the leadership of the Liberal party and the various pretenders were marshalling their political forces for the war of succession, John Diefenbaker rose on the floor of the House and delivered some typically scathing broadsides at the lot of them. He then left for a Caribbean cruise. I wondered at the time how the old warrior, for whom politics had always been a totally consuming passion, could ever unwind long enough to enjoy such a diversion as a Caribbean cruise.

THE SCENE:

Seagull cries . . . the blast of a ship's whistle . . . the chatter of passengers lounging in deck chairs.

PASSENGER *(Very British)*: By Jove, sir! Just smell the tang of that salt air. Nothing quite like it, what? Miles and miles of ocean as far as the eye can see and nothing to do but sit back and enjoy it. I say, if our friends back home could see us now they'd be green with envy.

DIEFENBAKER: Well I certainly don't envy Green. . . .

PASSENGER: What?

DIEFENBAKER: . . . or any of those Liberal contenders for that matter.

PASSENGER: I'm sorry . . . I'm not quite sure I. . . .

DIEFENBAKER: Uh . . . they're going to have a lot of trouble with that Medicare. Mind you, I warned them. I said to them . . . I said. . . .

PASSENGER: Yes, by Jove, this certainly beats shovelling snow or pushing one's car out of a drift. I must say it's always pleasant to leave those Canadian winters behind.

DIEFENBAKER: Ah, yes . . . yes indeed . . . and all the rest of them as well.

PASSENGER: I . . . I beg your pardon?

DIEFENBAKER: Winters . . . Martin . . . Sharp . . . they're all the same you know. Yes, they're going to have a real mess on their hands with that Medicare. I warned them, of course. I said to them. . . .

PASSENGER: Uh . . . yes . . . uh . . . I . . . uh . . . I love the Caribbean Islands. Terribly fond of them but I do believe my favourite is Martinique.

DIEFENBAKER: Well, of course, as far as I'm concerned you can keep Martinique. Yes and you can keep Pearsonique, Hellyerique and the whole lot. They're all the same . . . all tarred with the same brush.

PASSENGER: I . . . uh . . . I've been coming to these islands down here for the past twenty years, you know. The thrill's always there. Never seem to lose their lustre, somehow.

DIEFENBAKER: Not like the Liberals. They certainly lost their Lester.

PASSENGER: I beg your pardon?

DIEFENBAKER: Oh, yes . . . and not a moment too soon. Well, I told him dozens of times on the floor of the House. . . .

PASSENGER: Look here, old boy, I'm afraid I don't quite. . . .

DIEFENBAKER: Lester, I said, why don't you quit . . . get out . . . give this country a chance.

PASSENGER: Uh . . . if you'll excuse me . . . uh . . . I think I'll just take a turn or two around the deck.

DIEFENBAKER: Uh, Turner too! Yes, you're quite right. I told *him* to get out. Naturally, he wouldn't listen to me. Oh, they're all the same. . . .

PASSENGER (*Desperately*): Deck Steward!

DIEFENBAKER: . . . all the same . . . they don't fool me . . . I remember once. . . .

PASSENGER: Steward! It's a bit distracting up here on the sundeck. I wonder if I might have my chair moved down to the engine-room.

TO ERR IS HUMAN

On the eve of the federal election, in June of 1968, Tommy Douglas flew to Regina for a speaking engagement. He was met at the airport by a delegation of cheering doctors, complete with band. They, of course, mistook him for one of the delegates to their Canadian Medical Association convention and when the mistake was discovered, the smiles soon turned to glum looks and even scowls for the very man who had initiated the idea of Medicare. Somehow, we just don't expect mistakes like that from the medical fraternity.

THE SCENE:

An operation is in progress in a Regina hospital.

MEDICAL STUDENT (*With reverent awe*): Doctor, I just want to say again it's awfully good of you to let me stand in on this one. I mean, like, I'm only in my third year at medical school so, boy oh boy, to get a chance to observe an operation like this with a man of your stature in the medical field. . . .

GRUFF DOCTOR: Hmmm. That's O.K. . . . Clamp . . . Suture . . . quickly!

MEDICAL STUDENT: Golly, this is worth a whole year of lectures just to watch the way you work, doctor.

GRUFF DOCTOR: Hmmm . . . Clean that up there, nurse . . . Press down . . . that's enough. *(To student)* This your first Caesarian section?

MEDICAL STUDENT: Yes, sir. Wow, what an experience!

GRUFF DOCTOR *(Low)*: O.K. . . . tie that off . . . forceps . . . *(To student)* Well, I must say this is going pretty smoothly in spite of my nerves. I haven't been so shaken up in quite a while.

STUDENT: Oh? What's the trouble, sir?

GRUFF DOCTOR: Well, I guess you read about it in the papers. You can't keep a thing like that from the press. A whole bunch of us went out to the airport yesterday to welcome some delegates to the CMA convention here.

STUDENT: Oh, yes, I . . . uh . . . I read that story.

GRUFF DOCTOR: How we could have made a dumb mistake like that is beyond me. Standing there like a bunch of idiots cheering and waving, bands playing . . . and who walks out but Judas Iscariot.

STUDENT: Judas Iscariot, sir?

GRUFF DOCTOR: Tommy Douglas! Mr. Medicare! The guy that sent us all out on strike back in '62.

STUDENT: Must have been very embarrassing.

GRUFF DOCTOR: Well, it'll be all over Canada. We'll be the laughing stock of . . . of . . . Geez! Of all the professions to make a mistake like that! Doctors! Traditionally renowned for cool thinking, level heads, rational behaviour, clear analytical minds. I just don't know how we could have done a thing like that! Oh . . . look . . . would you like to give me a hand here?

STUDENT: Could I really?

GRUFF DOCTOR: Sure. Just take it easy . . . gently does it . . . that's it . . . O.K. . . . There we go.

STUDENT *(Voice quavering)*: Boy, I'll never forget this as long as I live!!

11

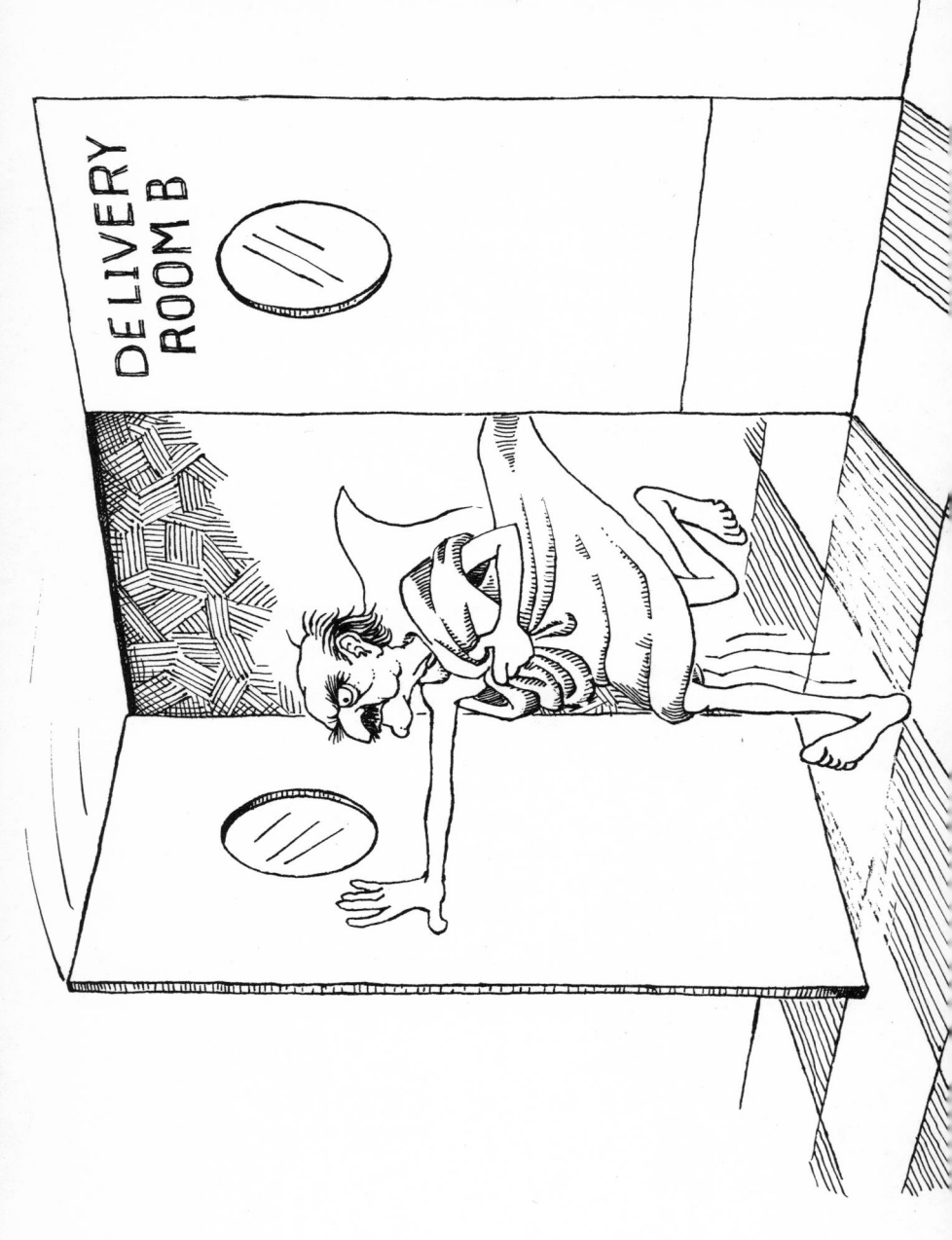

GRUFF DOCTOR: All right now . . . that's got it . . . good, good! Well, Mrs. Murch . . . Mrs. Murch! *(Gentle slapping of face)* It's all over now Mrs. Murch, and guess what we've got for you here. I'm going to leave the little fella right here beside you . . . yes, you can hold him . . . while I go and get washed up. *(Softening)* You know, son, no matter how professionally objective you might think you are, these moments really get to you. It's the quintessence of motherhood when that fragile little life, which they've so patiently and lovingly carried all those long months, is finally lying there beside them.

NURSE *(Running in to operating room)*: Doctor! Doctor!

GRUFF DOCTOR: What is it, nurse?

NURSE: Is Mrs. Murch your patient?

GRUFF DOCTOR: She certainly is.

NURSE: Well, they've got her in O.R. 3!

GRUFF DOCTOR: What?

NURSE: They've been waiting for you all morning, doctor!

GRUFF DOCTOR: What?

NURSE: They've been paging you all over the hospital!

GRUFF DOCTOR: But nurse, I've just this moment . . . oh, no! Oh, my gawd!

[*He rushes out. Feeble whining protests are heard from the limp form on the operating table.*]

NURSE: There now, Mr. Smiley. It's all right. It's all right.

PATIENT *(Barely audible)*: Nurse . . . take . . . take this . . . out . . . of here.

NURSE: Certainly, sir . . . don't you worry about a thing . . . *(Up)* Will someone get this appendix off Mr. Smiley's chest! It's all right Mr. Smiley, we just made a little mistake . . . the . . . uh . . . the doctor was . . . uh . . . he was expecting someone else.

As the Tory political machine girded its loins to fight the 1968 federal election with Bob Stanfield, the burning question was whether or not the old king, John Diefenbaker, still smouldering and resentful over his recent deposition, would support the new prince regent. When the Chief agreed to ride beside Stanfield in a Saskatoon motorcade, the Tory planners were delighted, taking this gesture to mean he was throwing his support behind Stanfield. But, with Dief, you can never always be that sure!

THE SCENE:

Cheering crowds . . . bands playing . . . as Stanfield and Diefenbaker drive together through the streets of Saskatoon in an open car.

DIEFENBAKER (*smiling and waving*): Hello there Alvin! . . . uh, how's the drugstore? . . . Eh? . . . uh, splendid . . . uh, glad to hear it, Alvin! Goomer! Almost missed you behind that lamp post . . . uh, wonderful to see you again. Did you ever get that hernia fixed . . . uh, wonderful Goomer . . . uh, splendid. (*Confidentially to* BOB) Uh, say Bob. . . .

STANFIELD: Um . . . uh . . . yes? . . . uh, what is it, John?

DIEFENBAKER: Well, Bob, I just thought it would be nice, as we drive past these vast throngs lining the streets of Saskatoon, if . . . uh . . . you could stand up here beside me and . . . uh . . . (*up full*) Uh, hello there Gerney! You're looking great! . . . (*Back to* BOB) Well . . . uh . . . smile and wave to all the friendly folk.

STANFIELD: Well . . . uh . . . John . . . um . . . if it's just the same to you . . . uh . . . I'd just as soon sit here in the back of the convertible and . . . uh . . . uh . . . work on my notes. I . . . uh . . . I've got a speech to give tomorrow.

DIEFENBAKER. Well now, Bob, I realize it's not your nature to grin like a Cheshire cat . . . uh, I'm not asking you to be a Mitchell Sharp . . . but do you think you might be able to manage . . . uh, for all these good people who've turned out to see us . . . uh, maybe even a tiny sort of Mona Lisa smile.

STANFIELD: Um . . . uh . . . I'm sorry, John . . . but I'd rather sit here and work on this speech.

DIEFENBAKER: Well, Bob, do you think you could possibly . . . (*up full*) Uh, Hello there Cyril . . . nice to see you again . . . uh, my goodness, are those all your children? . . . Uh, just watch it, Cyril, you might do yourself out of a seat in the car! Uh, hee hee hee. (*back to* BOB) Uh, do you think, Bob, you could possibly manage a small gesture of warmth . . . perhaps a little wave. Oh, I'm not asking for any theatrical cartwheels out there on the hood of the convertible, Bob, but perhaps a subdued little wave along the lines of that given by Her Majesty.

STANFIELD: Uh . . . John . . . uh . . . I'd just as soon not.

DIEFENBAKER: Uh, you know Bob. Uh, there's something bothering you. I can spot it.

STANFIELD: Oh, no . . . uh . . . nothing . . . nothing at all, John.

DIEFENBAKER: Ah, yes, Bob. Something's troubling you. The old effervescence just isn't there. Certainly, I've done everything I can, Bob. I agreed to meet with you publicly. I shook your hand for the photographers. I even arranged for this limousine so we could ride together. Now, out with it Bob. Uh, if you can't discuss this openly with me, then who *can* you discuss it with.

STANFIELD: Well . . . uh . . . it's just a small thing, John. Normally, I wouldn't give it a second thought . . . it wouldn't bother me at all . . . but I guess the nerves are a little taut . . . pressure of the campaign and all.

DIEFENBAKER: What is it, Bob?

STANFIELD: Promise you won't think I'm being peevish or temperamental.

DIEFENBAKER: Uh, certainly not, Bob!

STANFIELD: Well, we still have about eighteen more blocks to drive . . . there'll be quite a few more people we have to pass . . . so I was just wondering . . .

DIEFENBAKER: Uh, yes Bob?

STANFIELD: Um . . . uh . . . for those last few blocks, do you suppose we could remove all those Trudeau signs from the sides of the convertible?

WHO STOLE YOUR HEART AWAY

In 1968 the world's first heart-transplant operation took place in South Africa. It was an operation which transcended that country's race laws. The white recipient went so far as to announce that he had no objections to receiving the heart of a black man. Apart from the medical possibilities the sociological implications were intriguing. A black heart in a white body. If the operation became commonplace it might help to bring about the long-awaited brotherhood of Man.

THE SCENE:

The tense, dramatic operating room back-ground of a large hospital.

REPORTER: This is Leslie Lovelace of the CBC. I'm going to have to lower my voice and deliver this report in hushed tones this morning because I'm standing here in the operating room of one of the largest hospitals in the United States. For the past hour now, I've been observing the surgical wizardry of Dr. Seth Butler, the foremost heart surgeon of Atlanta, Georgia. He is, at this very moment, completing the successful transplant of a Negro heart into the body of a white citizen of Atlanta. The surgical team is just closing now and if I can move over a bit closer . . . oh, excuse me Dr. Butler . . . if you could spare a moment I would like to ask. . . .

DR. BUTLER: Hold it, fella. Just you wait a itty-bitty second till ah git this tied off hyah. Theah! That does it. Now you just fire away.

REPORTER: Dr. Butler this operation is now becoming routine. Does it still present major difficulties?

DR. BUTLER: Well, now, let me tell ya, it's no piece of cake. We always up aginst the problem of the human body rejectin' any foreign organ. Course, in this part of the world that problem is a mite aggravated.

REPORTER: How do you get around this rejection phenomenon?

DR. BUTLER: Well, we jist keep tryin'. Had a patient last week . . . body rejected the heart. We just kept pickin' it up off the floor and puttin' it back in. Course, by and large, we findin' less and less of that sort of thing. Here in Atlanta, Georgia, white bodies are startin' to accept niggrah hearts.

REPORTER: Do you feel there's any social significance to this?

DR. BUTLER: Ah sure as hell do. So far this yeah, ah put twenty-five niggrah hearts into white bodies. Done three of em jist this mornin'. Ah wanna tell you we got folks walkin' round the streets of Atlanta . . . white folks, leaders of the community . . . that have got niggrah hearts beatin' inside of em. Ah feel the more we git of this kinda thing goin' on, the more folks is gonna realize that, when ya git right down to it, we all brothers . . . we all children of God and colour is only skin deep.

REPORTER: You think all this will bring about a change in the Southerner's attitude toward the black?

DR. BUTLER: Mistah, as this operation becomes more and more routine . . . as all these hyah niggrah hearts git put into white bodies, you gonna see a end to all these centuries of injustice. . . .

NURSE (*calling from door of operating room*): Oh, doctor?

DR. BUTLER: ... of ... of ... mistreatment. ...

NURSE: Doctor!

DR. BUTLER: ... of exploitation of the niggrah. ...

NURSE: Doctor ... please!

DR. BUTLER: Yeah, what is it nurse?

NURSE: Doctor, those three patients in Ward A.

DR. BUTLER: Now, don't you go fussin' your pretty little head 'bout them, nurse.

NURSE: But doctor ... those three Negro patients. ...

DR. BUTLER: It's all right, honey ... I'll look after them.

NURSE: But doctor ... they ... they've vanished!

DR. BUTLER: It's all right nurse. Now don't you fret.

NURSE: But I can't find them anywhere and they were scheduled for surgery this afternoon.

DR. BUTLER: I know nurse ... everything's fine ... don't you worry.

NURSE: There were two tonsillectomy cases. ...

DR. BUTLER: Yeah, pretty far gone ... looked awful bad.

NURSE: ... and one hernia case.

DR. BUTLER: That's right ... just about the worst ah've seen ... looked terminal to me.

NURSE: But doctor, where on earth could they have gone. Shouldn't we. ...

DR. BUTLER: It's all right nurse. Now jist quit shoutin' and clear outta heah ... no problem ... everything's fine, ya heah?...

THE DEN MOTHER

When Prince Andrew, younger brother of Prince Charles, joined the fifth Marlborough cub pack it was decided that the weekly meetings would be held at Andrew's place, Buckingham Palace. His fellow cubs were delighted at this choice of a den but can you imagine the dilemma of protocol imposed upon the cub leader.

THE SCENE:

The gleeful shouts of young cubs at a typical meeting.

CUBMASTER: I say, boys . . . not too much noise now. Let's all play up and play the game. After all we must respect this home in which we've been allowed to hold our meeting. Oh, Leslie! What a perfectly smashing knot you've tied there. That's a clove-hitch. Very nicely done. Nigel! Oh, Nigel! I'm simply delighted with that lovely fire you have going over there. What? Did it with only two sticks? Splendid! But look, could you possibly move it off the oriental rug and onto the marble foyer there? Now, chaps, if I could have your attention for just a moment. Our meeting will be drawing to a close very shortly and we shall be holding our usual closing ceremonies. Now I should like . . . . (*resounding and impressive fanfare*) Oh, my goodness . . . oh dear me . . . Boys! Not a sound! Everyone at attention, your two fingers up smartly just touching the peaks of your little caps! That's it. (*Clears throat nervously, then to the visitor*) Ah . . . good evening Mrs. Mountbatt . . . er . . . won't you come in and join us? You're most welcome to watch our little closing ceremony. Boys, I'm delighted to announce that we have a very special visitor . . . Her Royal Brittanic Maj . . . uh, no, no, that's not quite right . . . uh . . . Boys, one of the mothers has dropped in this evening to see us. So nice to see the boys' moms taking an interest.

I hardly need tell you, boys, that this is the kind lady who had the Bovril and bickies sent down to us to make our weekly meetings that much more enjoyable. Now then, boys, if you'll all form a big circle around the flag . . . Nigel, I think we'll let you hold the flag this evening . . . and we'll sing our closing song. Oh, just hold on a moment. Perhaps it would be nice if Andrew stood in the centre of the circle and all the boys knelt down and saluted him with our cub salute. Nigel, perhaps you could also give him the flag to hold. You can hold it some other night. Now then, are we all ready for our closing song? I'm quite sure that tonight we'll sing out with great feeling and emotion because not only is it a wonderfully moving song that has seen our country through many historic moments but indeed, boys, the very lady to whom it refers is standing right here with us. All right boys . . . one . . . two . . . three. (chorus of piping cubs)

God save your gracious mom,
Long live your noble mom,
God save your mom.
Send her victorious,
Happy and glorious,
Long to reign over us,
God save your mom!

BENEFITS FORGOT

The first Canadian Constitutional Conference, held back in February of 1968, ended on a much more optimistic note than our last one. Prime Minister Pearson was described by the press as "pink-cheeked and smiling" as he told the ten provincial premiers

*that fifty years hence, a new generation would look
back on them and say of them "They builded better
than they knew!" I wonder if he took into account the
new trends in education which would be moulding
the minds of that new generation.*

THE SCENE:

A typical Canadian classroom of the early twenty-first
century.

LADY TEACHER: Now children, please quieten down! After all
we do have a history class to get on with here. Surely, if
the Board of Education is willing to pay all of you $25 a
day for just coming here the least you can do is fulfill
your end of the bargain. Now I have a very pleasant surprise for you. Without telling you, I wrote away to the
President's Printer in Ottawa . . . he used to be called the
Queen's Printer years ago when we had self-government.
Now I want you to look at this lovely old photograph that
I received in the mail. Study it carefully and tell me who
these men are seated around the table. We have to go
back quite a few years for this one. I'll give you a little
clue. This man here . . . the one with the smile and the
pink cheeks . . . he's the leader and these other ten men are
his helpers. Now let's get those thinking caps on and find
out who these men were.

KIDS (*listlessly*): The Last Supper.

TEACHER: No, no, *no*! Not the Last Supper. Not that far back,
children. Now study the faces. These men lived about fifty
years ago and among them they held a lot of power.

KIDS (*listlessly*): The Mafia.

TEACHER: No, children, no! Goodness gracious! These are the
men who attended the famous Constitutional Conference
way back in 1968. That's Mr. Pearson there and those
others are the provincial premiers. Now then, what do we

always say . . . what familiar line do we always use . . . when we look at these men?

KIDS (*listlessly*): If you can't say anything nice about someone, don't say. . . .

TEACHER: No, no, no! We do *not* say that. When we see this picture we always stand up, place our hands over our hearts and say: "They builded better than they knew!"

KIDS (*suddenly animated*): Builded! ! ! !

TEACHER: Yes, builded.

KIDS: You used bad grammar! ! ! !

TEACHER: Children, please. I was simply. . . .

KIDS: You used bad grammar! You used bad grammar!

TEACHER: Children! Listen to me please. "Builded" is simply what we call an archaic expression. You see, some words. . . .

ARNOLD: Teacher?

TEACHER: Yes, Arnold?

ARNOLD: Ten years ago, when the Board of Education gave us students the right to hire, fire and discipline teachers they built better than they knew. As president of our student council, I would like to inform you that you are fired for using bad grammar.

KIDS (*all chanting with relentless finality*): You're fired! You're fired!

TEACHER (*with mounting hysteria over the Orwellian chant*): No, no . . . please children . . . give me another chance . . . please . . . I beg of you . . . please!

Hospitals will soon be able to keep a watchful ear on heart patients even after they've been discharged. A monitoring device, implanted in the patient's chest, will enable him to go about his daily routine while the hospital listens in electronically to a sort of transmitted progress report.

THE SCENE:

The expensively furnished apartment of business executive J.W. Wardell where, in a milieu of soft music, subdued lighting and liquor, an earnest attempt is being made by J.W. to befriend a young office secretary.

J.W.: Heavens, Miss Willington, I hadn't even noticed how low your drink is getting. Here, let me just touch it up.

MISS W.: Oh, gee, J.W. I think one drink is really my limit.

J.W.: Nonsense, Miss Willington, one little drink isn't enough for a fully grown . . . er . . . for a growing girl like you. Let me just freshen it.
[*Sound of excessive and prolonged pouring.*]

MISS W.: Please, J.W. I don't think you can get any more in that glass. It's going all over my lap.

J.W.: Oh, I'm sorry.

MISS W.: Gee, you certainly have a lovely place here.

J.W.: All the lovelier, Miss Willington, when graced by your presence. You know, it's very strange. Watching you around the office this past year or so. . . .

MISS W.: I just started last week, J.W.

J.W.: Watching you around the office this past week . . . or so . . . I never dreamed that behind that facade of the horn-rimmed glasses . . . the hair drawn back into a rather severe

23

bun . . . I never dreamed that behind all th
charming . . . I might even say exciting . . . young, very
MISS W.: That's awfully sweet of you, J.W. I just want you to
know how groovy I felt when you took the time to find
out I was interested in stamps and offered to let me look
through your albums this evening.

J.W.: Oh? Oh! Oh, yes. Yes, of course, my stamps.

MISS W.: I sure would like to see them.

J.W.: Well, they . . . uh . . .they'll keep, Miss Willington. After
all, stamps aren't like eggs . . . they won't go rotten.
(*nervous laugh*) They're . . . uh . . . they're in the den as a
matter of fact. By golly, you look uncomfortable sitting
there on the edge of the chesterfield. Why don't you just
lean back and rest your head against my chest?

M.SS W.: Well, I . . . I . . . well all right. Ouch!!

J.W.: Something wrong, Miss Willington?

MISS W.: Something sharp just stuck into my head. Was that a
ball-point pen?

J.W.: No, no. It's . . . uh . . . it's my . . . uh . . . it's my transistor
radio . . . ha-ha.

MISS W.: Golly, that really stung. Could you take it out, J.W.?

J.W.: No, as a matter of fact I can't.

MISS W.: You can't remove your transistor radio?

J.W.: I'm afraid not, Miss Willington. This is going to sound a
little crazy, ha-ha, but it's . . . uh . . . it's under my skin . . .
it's sewn in.

MISS W.: You have your transistor radio sewn under your skin?

J.W.: Well . . . ha-ha . . . you know me. I'd lose my head if it
wasn't nailed on. No, seriously, Miss Willington, I've lost
about six of the darn things in the past year. Always
leaving them around. So I finally decided to have one sewn
into my skin . . . it just . . . uh . . . it just seemed the sensible
thing to do. But getting back to what I was saying, I
really think you're an exciting woman, Miss Willington
and . . . uh . . . well. . . . (*His breathing becomes noticeably
stentorian.*) . . . I just happen to feel that certain rare
moments are Heaven sent . . . sort of fore-ordained. They
. . . they come once in a lifetime and we've got to seize

those moments. We've got to answer that hot call of the blood. . . . We've got to . . . we've . . . what I'm trying to say. . . . (*The phone rings jarringly leaving him suspended in a strangulated passion. He grabs it and barks angrily*) Who the hell is this! The what? The Victoria General! Well you've got your nerve phoning at this hour of the night. I've paid you guys my pound of flesh. I don't owe you one cent . . . not one red. . . . The beeps are what? Coming 470 to the minute! My God. No . . . no. No, I am *not* playing squash! I am *not* moving furniture. Well, frankly, I don't think it's any of your damn business! That's right! (*The phone is slammed down.*) Where was I, Miss Willington?

MISS W.: You were saying, J.W., how we have to make the most of each magic moment.

J.W.: What? Oh! ! Yes, yes. That's right. I feel we should put every moment to good use, Miss Willington . . . because in that way we can contribute . . . each in his own small way . . . to . . . uh . . . to the common good of the company. I further feel, Miss Willington, that we should bring to our job each morning, a . . . a . . . a clear head and a well-rested body. May I call you a cab?

MISS W.: But golly, it's only nine-thirty, J.W. and I haven't even seen your stamps yet.

J.W.: Uh . . . some other time, Miss Willington. I had no idea it was so late. I'm sorry . . . I . . . uh . . . I'll call you, Miss Willington.

SHARING THE LOAD

I wonder if anything has been done yet to implement a rather good suggestion from the Ontario Department of Health. About a year ago it was officially announced that the standard of medical care could be appreciably raised if hard-pressed and harried doctors had some of the routine trivia taken off their hands. Nurses could look after the minor routine work leaving doctors free to concentrate on the more important side of medical care.

THE SCENE:

A hospital room. The doctor has just arrived having been summoned by the nurse.

DOCTOR (*with a weary sigh*): Yes, nurse, what is it?

NURSE: I'm terribly sorry to bother you, doctor, I know you're just run off your feet these days but I think the patient is ready for you now.

DOCTOR: You looked after that little detail did you?

NURSE: Well, I did the best I could, doctor.

DOCTOR: I must say it makes quite a difference to be able to unload some of these piddling little time-wasters on you nurses. Now just what have you done here?

NURSE: Well, when you called me in to relieve you I found Mr. Woods in what appeared to be deep catatonic coma. I suspected cardiac arrest but decided first of all to run an electro-encephalogram.

DOCTOR: Good . . . just what I would have done.

NURSE: No brain damage had occurred so I then decided on open-heart surgery.

DOCTOR: Good thinking.

NURSE: Hooking the patient up to the heart-lung machine, I excised a small malfunctioning segment near the aorta

which seemed to give strong evidence of arterial-sclerotic impairment.

DOCTOR: I think I might have preferred an enema but that's neither here nor there.

NURSE: I grafted a plastic section in order to by-pass the diseased area and then imbedded a pace-maker just below the valve. His breathing has resumed and his eyes are beginning to focus, so if you'd like to take over again, doctor.

DOCTOR: Thanks, nurse, it's a great help to know that when work piles up and pressure starts to mount you girls can step in and take some of these pedestrian, run-of-the-mill details off the hands of us hard-pressed doctors. You may think it's just a trifling and insignificant contribution but it does leave us free to concentrate on the more demanding and, of course, essential aspects of medicine.

NURSE (*as she exists from room*): It was a pleasure helping out, doctor. Goodbye.

[*door slams.*]

DOCTOR (*lifting patient's eyelid with thumb*): Now then, Mr. Lead-Swinger, as I was pointing out just before you pulled that rather childish psychosomatic cardiac arrest, your bill is now around $3500 and so far you've only paid a paltry $300. Now we're going to have to do better than that, aren't we? Now there's no point turning blue in the face. I'm not going to be put off by cheap histrionics. Will you tell me once and for all what you're planning to do to repay me for the hours of medical skill and professional care I've lavished on you. Now no more of this dilly-dallying ... I'm a busy man ... overworked ... hard pressed ... are you listening to me? ...

NEVER, IN THE HISTORY OF POSTAL STRIKES...

The chaos and confusion expected from the general postal strike which hit Britain in January, 1970, was fortunately minimized thanks to such private initiative as the former World War Two dispatch rider who organized a corps of private posties on motorcycles.

THE SCENE:

Rush hour at Piccadilly Circus, London.

ANNOUNCER: This is Nigel Thrimbleby of the BBC speaking to you from Piccadilly Circus. Beside me is Harry Atkins, one of several enterprising citizens here in Britain who have inaugurated private postal services during these days of national crisis brought on by the postal strike. Harry, you're a former RAF fighter pilot are you not?

HARRY: That's right, chum. Like a lot of other blokes durin' the war, I was trained at guv'ment expense to fly a aircraft and I feel that, durin' this emergency, the least wot we can do is offer the guv'ment our special skills in its hour of need. Like, you 'ave this 'ere former dispatch rider wot's deliverin' mail on motor-bike. There's also another bloke 'ere in London, former artillery man, wot's usin' a old 88-millimetre gun to lob parcels from 'ere up to Newcastle.

ANNOUNCER: Isn't that extraordinary!

HARRY: Yes, well, I mean, 'e 'ad a spot of back luck at first ... wounded quite a few people up there 'is first couple of go's. I mean, we're all a bit rusty. But they tell me 'e got the range all right after a bit. Lobbin' them in now wif no trouble at all.

ANNOUNCER: What, exactly, is your contribution, Mr. Atkins?

HARRY: Well, shortly after the war, I 'ad the foresight to purchase me old Spitfire from the guv'ment ... got it through

war surplus . . . been keepin' it tidy and shipshape ever since.

ANNOUNCER: Jove! How very fortunate. So, now, you're able to fly to various parts of Britain delivering mail?

HARRY: Oh no! I don't never go outside of London.

ANNOUNCER: You deliver mail in London . . . by Spitfire?

HARRY: Well, I mean, she's been twenty-five years sittin' in me garage. I've fussed over that old Rolls Royce Merlin engine like a ruddy mum wif me tin of oil and me spanner . . . but I can't get it off the ground . . . can't get it airborne, like!

ANNOUNCER: But how on earth do you deliver mail?

HARRY: Well, it still taxis nicely so I just drive the old Spitfire about the London streets . . . pickin' up mail 'ere . . . droppin' it off there. Bit of a tight squeeze now and then . . . specially right 'ere in Piccadilly Circus.

ANNOUNCER: Yes, it does seem a rather tight traffic circle and frightfully congested!

HARRY: Well, I mean, I'm petrified every time I 'ave to come through 'ere . . . 'ave to keep checkin' me wing tip to make sure I 'aven't emasculated the statute of Eros. Most of the time I just keeps me eyes shut, crosses me fingers and yells out: "Mind your bleedin' 'eads!"

[*The chorus of angry horns grows louder.*]

HARRY: Oh, shut your face . . . the lot of you! Hi, you! Stuff it, mate!

ANNOUNCER: Well, thank you, Mr. Atkins. I won't detain you. There seem to be quite a few motors piling up behind you, here!

HARRY: Oh, don't you mind that lot! There's a few rotten apples in every barrel. The important thing is to get the mail through! Avoid, at all costs, chaos, congestion, snafus and general pandemonium.

[*The surly drivers begin to vocalize.*]

VARIOUS VOICES: 'Ere, you! Move that Spitfire . . . pack it out of 'ere! . . . Will you kindly remove that beastly thing. I can't get my Bentley through! . . . Come on you, get that bloody great monster out of 'ere!

HARRY: Aaarrrhhh! Stow it, will you! Yes, I know you lot . . .
soon as this bleedin' strike's over, you'll be the first to
shake me 'and and say: "Never, in the 'istory of postal
strikes, was so much owed by so many to so few!"

ABSTINENCE MAKES THE HEART GROW FONDER

*In the Fall of 1970, Russian smokers learned from an
item in Pravda that there was now scientific evidence
that heavy smoking in males produces changes in
their sex hormones. These changes could cause men
as young as thirty to lose interest in sex.*

THE SCENE:

A big, strapping Russian sits in his Moscow apartment, inhaling luxuriously his Black Sobranie. The
phone rings.

Hallo! Da,da . . . ees Vladimir speaking. Aaahhh! How
good for hear your voice Alexei! Da . . . has been long time!
Dees evening? am doing nawtheeng . . . sure . . . sure . . .
dees sound like good fun! Da . . . could be ready . . . height
o'clock, for sure . . . would henjoy beeg night on town
weeth old friend! Dreenks? . . . da! . . . Bolshoi? . . . da, da!
. . . fine deener, cigars, lots wodka your place later? . . .
sure, you bet Alexei! Look forward for see you! . . . You in-
wite *who?* . . . Olga, Tanya, Sascha, Maria, Katrina and
Anastasia? Ah, ees too bad, Alexei . . . nyet, nyet . . . dees
cannot be. What our Russian scientists say ees only too

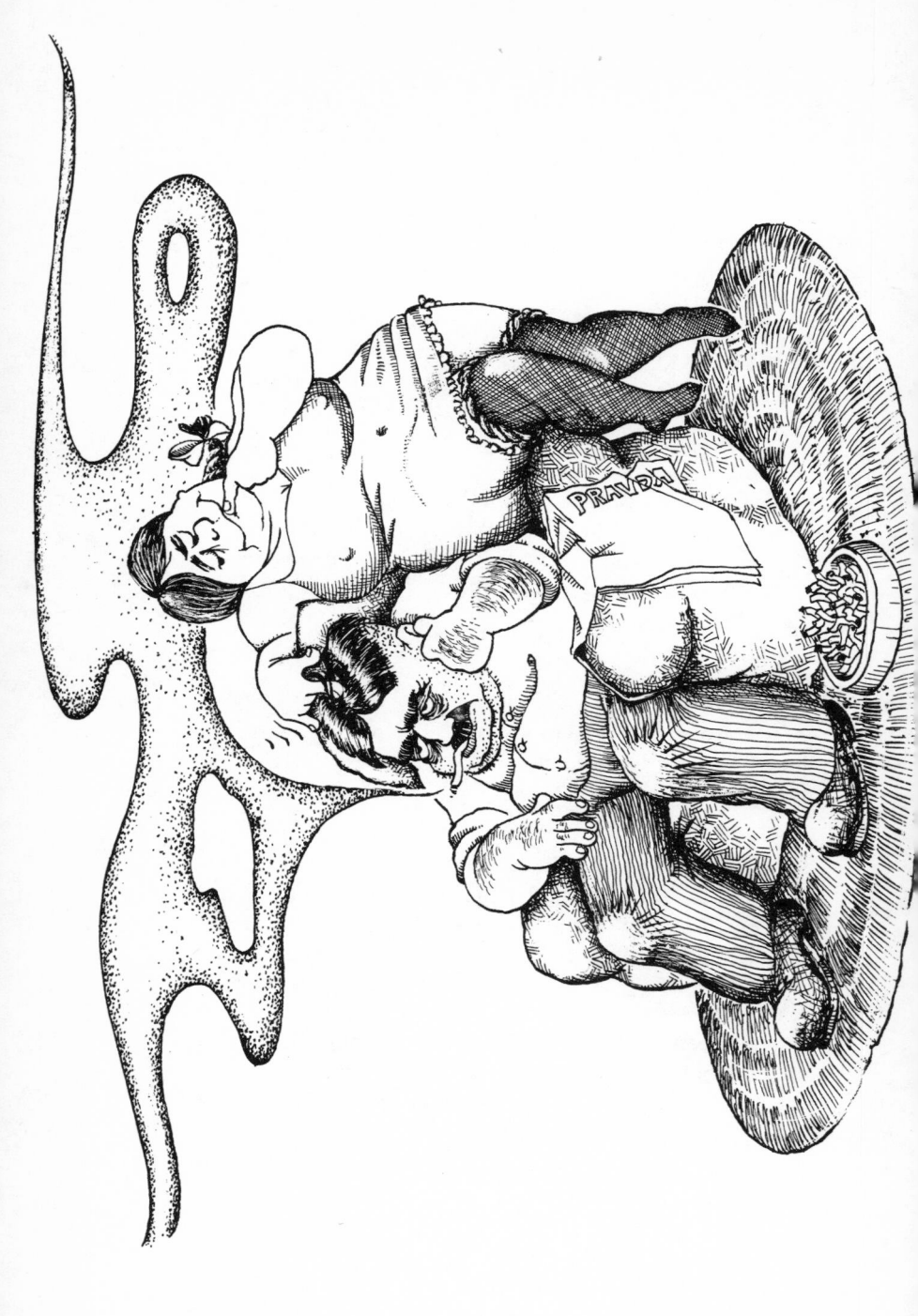

true . . . da . . . you remember what heavy smoker I have been? For thirty years smoke two packages each day Black Sobranie . . . da . . . da . . . ees wery embarrassing to say dees to you . . . but . . . now for me . . . sex ees too much . . . would not be able for sex . . . four, maybe, . . . even five . . . but sex . . . nyet! You can get rid of Anastasia? . . . da . . . da . . . keep other five? . . . Ees good . . . ees good . . . dees be O.K.

NO NEED TO PANIC

No politician ever played things as cool as Pierre Elliott Trudeau and never was his sangfroid more evident than in the FLQ crisis during the fall of 1970. Whenever Opposition Leader, Robert Stanfield, questioned him in the House and expressed concern over the suspension of civil liberties and the presence of fully-armed combat troops in the streets of Ottawa he always managed to minimize things and make you feel like "a bleeding heart" for feeling any concern.

THE SCENE:

The Canadian House of Commons

STANFIELD: Mr. Speaker . . . uh . . . I . . . uh . . . I would like to rise now and . . . uh . . . and. . . .
SPEAKER (*bored*): And go to Innisfree?
STANFIELD: Uh . . . no . . . I would like to rise now on a question of privilege and ask the Prime Minister just how far he

plans to go toward placing this country on what is beginning to look like a wartime footing.

TRUDEAU: Mr. Speaker, I would like to remind the Honourable leader of the Opposition that what we have done so far can hardly be construed as placing Canada on a wartime footing. Really, I can't help feeling that if we were to place a barrel under all these bleeding hearts, the Red Cross wouldn't have to hold any more blood clinics.

STANFIELD: Well then, perhaps the Prime Minister will tell us why so many armed troops are being brought in from Petawawa.

TRUDEAU: The only reason we are using the military is so that they can take over the normal duties of regular civilian organizations thus enabling the latter to quietly go about the task of ensuring public safety.

STANFIELD: You mean the soldiers aren't being brought in for this purpose.

TRUDEAU: Certainly not. They will simply go from door to door selling cookies and collecting old newspapers so that the Boy Scouts and Girl Guides of this city will be free to carry out certain little precautions for the common good of all citizens . . . little things . . . good turns you might call them such as laying anti-submarine nets across the Gulf of St. Lawrence, floating barrage balloons over the House of Commons, re-locating the West Coast Japanese and confiscating their property *et cetera, et cetera....*

[*Thumping of desks and cheers from government benches.*]

NOTHING CAN STOP THE ARMY AIR CORPS

Some people are born famous, others have fame thrust upon them. I suppose you could put Captain Susan R. Struck, United States Air Force, in that latter category. In October, 1970, when she made the headlines, she was eight months along the way to becoming the first commissioned airforce officer anywhere to give birth while on active duty. Susan, unmarried, planned to put the child up for adoption and "make a career with the Air Force."

THE SCENE:

A platoon of air force trainees march across the drill square under the watchful eye of Captain Susan Struck.

SUSAN: Hup-two . . . hup-two . . . keep those shoulders back . . . hup-two . . . eyes facing front . . . hup-two . . . hup-two . . . Squaaaaad . . . halt! Stand easy! Those who are weak-willed may smoke!

COLONEL (*approaching*): Well . . . good morning, Captain Struck.

SUSAN: Oh . . . good morning, colonel. My, I'm so pleased the Air Force is letting me stay on with them.

COLONEL: Well, we're all delighted to have you . . . er . . . perhaps I could put that a little differently. We're all delighted to see you staying with the air force. By the way, how far along are you?

SUSAN (*proudly*): Three years, sir!

COLONEL: No . . . uh . . . I meant in your . . . uh . . . pregancy, captain.

SUSAN: Oh, that! Um . . . let's see . . . just starting my ninth month.

COLONEL: You're . . . uh . . . still planning to put your baby up for adoption?

SUSAN: Well, I must admit, colonel, as the big day gets closer I'm having second thoughts about giving it away.

COLONEL: Good . . . splendid!

SUSAN: I felt it would be more in keeping with service life if I raffled it off in the mess.

COLONEL: Captain . . . one or two small points I wanted to bring up with you. The M.O. tells me you were issued with pills about a year ago.

SUSAN: That's right, sir.

COLONEL: He further tells me that you never bothered taking them.

SUSAN: Well, no colonel, I thought you only took cyanide pills if you fell into enemy hands.

COLONEL: That big red one was the cyanide pill, captain. The other little white ones you were supposed to take every day just in case you might fall into . . . well . . . uh . . . friendly hands. Now the other point concerned this parade square drill, captain. You're doing a good job. Don't be afraid to yell at these men. Demand one hundred per cent of them. If those heads aren't erect and those shoulders aren't back, you get right after them. However . . . uh . . . one small point. . . .

SUSAN: Sir?

COLONEL: I'd . . . uh . . . I'd soft pedal this business of keeping their tummies in!

UNEASY LIES THE HEAD

An English newspaper, the London Sun, *reported in November, 1970, that so far that year Her Majesty and Prince Philip had lost about two and a half million dollars playing the stock market.*

Mr. and Mrs. Average Londoner are sitting in front of their TV set on Christmas morning, 1970. Though Her Majesty's Christmas message has just concluded, the strains of "The Queen" still issue forth from the darkened screen.

PRIMROSE: Come on then, luv, 'ave another cup of tea. It'll make you feel better.

ALFIE (*morosely*): I don't want no tea! I just feel rotten . . . shockin'. Turn that bleedin' telly off, will you?
[*The strains of "The Queen" suddenly stop as the telly is turned off.*]

PRIMROSE: Now then, luv, there's no need to make such a fuss.

ALFIE: No bleedin' need you say? For forty years, I've been draggin' meself out of bed on a Christmas morning . . . never missed a year . . . to listen to them Christmas messages. I used to 'ear her granddad do it . . . George V. Then her father . . . George VI. But I've never 'eard the likes of that one. It was all over in four seconds!

PRIMROSE: Well, you must admit, Alfie, she did look lovely!

ALFIE: It's not 'ow she looked . . . it's wot she said . . . shocked me out of ten years of me life, she did!

PRIMROSE: Oh come on now, Alfie! You're so oldfashioned. I mean she's been sendin' out the same old Christmas message year after year. Must have been terribly borin' for 'er. You know wot they say . . . a change is as good as a rest! Personally, I found it quite original and refreshing . . . I mean quoting like that from Charles Dickens.

ALFIE: When Britain and the Commonwealth settle in front of the telly on a Christmas morning, breathless with expectation as they wait for their Queen to wish them a Merry Christmas . . . at that long-awaited moment when that familiar, radiant smile is about to fill us wif 'ope and inspiration . . . it's a bit of a shock to see 'er lean forward and snap "Christmas 'Umbug!" at the camera, and then bog off!

PRIMROSE: Oh, now Alfie! After all, she's only 'uman. 'Ow would you like to drop two and a 'alf million on the stock market? I'd 'ate to think of wot you'd say to the Commonwealth!

ALFIE: No excuse.

PRIMROSE: I'm quite sure you wouldn't be blowin' kisses and yellin' "Merry Christmas."

ALFIE: Shockin' . . . it's the end of an era!

PRIMROSE: I think she managed very well to come on at all . . . I'd be cryin' me bleedin' eyes out!

ALFIE: Christmas 'Umbug! I mean if she's going to come out with somefink like that on a Christmas morning she should at least try to make amends by sendin' around a big fat goose to the lot of us!!

THE FALLEN IDOL

Lex Barker, the 50-year-old movie Tarzan, who made a career of wrestling lions, crocodiles and gorillas was hospitalized in November, 1970. Tarzan had broken two ribs when he was shooting a movie scene and fell off a middle-aged horse.

THE SCENE:

An excited cluster of middle-aged nurses stand in the hospital corridor outside Tarzan's room.

NURSE ONE: They tell me he'll be going home tomorrow. His ribs are all healed. Of course, he always had terrific recuperative powers.

NURSE TWO: Oh, my yes! Do you remember that time when the big lion took a swipe at him and ripped his chest open . . . blood all over the place . . . you could almost see his lungs. But, would you believe it, one of the apes licked the wound and he was up and around in about five minutes! Gee, it's going to be so dull around here when he leaves!

NURSE THREE: I'll never forget that time he fought to the death with that big ugly eight-foot gorilla who'd fallen in love with Jane! Tarzan . . . or Lex, I should say . . . finally took the gorilla's head under his arm and cracked it. You could hear it all over the theatre! Gee, I just can't bear the thought of his leaving!

NURSE FOUR: Will you ever forget that yell he used to come out with? . . . the triumphant cry of the bull ape! Lex would plant one foot on the chest of his defeated adversary, throw his head back and, mercy! ! ! It would send goose pimples all over your body! It was so spinetingling . . . so primitive and brutish . . . so basically virile! Every day this week when I've gone into his room to give him a pill or take out the bedpan I've coaxed and pleaded with him to let me hear that sound again, but he wouldn't do it. Just so darn modest. I only wish. . . .

[*A series of brutish virile and primitive yells barrel suddenly out of Tarzan's room.*]

NURSE FOUR: My God . . . he's doing it! Quick, girls . . . come on!

[*Breathless, they all burst into the room.*]

DOCTOR: Gosh, all I did was try to take the tape off his ribs and all hell broke loose! He's going berserk! Somebody get a tranquilizer . . . quick! If we don't quieten this guy down, we're gonna have him for six more weeks with a double hernia! Wow . . . I've never seen a pain threshold as low as this guy's! ! !

THE WINTER GAMES PEOPLE PLAY

When the city of Saskatoon, Saskatchewan, under-took to host the 1970 Winter Games it created an entire manmade mountain on the flat prairie terrain. But the enterprising ingenuity didn't end there. Games Manager, Earle Bowman, managed to scrounge one of Eaton's old stores out there. Campers and trailers were moved into the three empty floors of the building and it served as an Olympic Village for the athletes.

THE SCENE:

An executive suite in Eaton's Toronto complex . . . heart of a mighty commercial empire.

JR. EXEC: Excuse me, R.J., this letter has just come in from Mr. Earle Bowman.

SR. EXEC: Bowman?

JR. EXEC: He's the manager of the Winter Games Society out in Saskatoon.

SR. EXEC: Oh, yes. The fellow who wheedled that old store out of us. Well, what does he want this time?

JR. EXEC: He was wondering about injured athletes. If they're returned to the store will Eaton's replace them with new ones or perhaps allow a cash refund?

SR. EXEC: Certainly not! No way! Give these people an inch and they'll take a mile. (*Phone rings.*) Get that, will you?

JR. EXEC: Hello, Eaton's Toronto store. Oh, hello there. How are you? Yes, you're coming in clear as a bell . . . pardon? . . . I see . . . you'll be getting in about a month early. Can we what? Well, I don't know. I'll have to check with R.J. Hold the line a second.

SR. EXEC: Is that that Bowman fellow again?

JR. EXEC: No. It's old Santa. He and Mrs. Claus and about

seventy-five elves plan to arrive in Toronto about a month early this year. Want to do some shopping and take in some of the night spots before we need them for our big parade. He was wondering if Eaton's would be willing to clear the displays out of its Yonge Street windows and let them all sleep there.

SR. EXEC: Preposterous! Not a chance! Tell him if he's coming in that early for our Christmas parade he can darn well pay for his own accommodation.

JR. EXEC: Hello, Santa? Look, I'm sorry but it's out of the question. Yes, I know we did this sort of thing for the Winter Games people out in Saskatoon but, gee, Santa if we did it for everybody we'd . . . now there's no need to fly off the handle . . . please don't jingle those bells in my ear. What? Santa, I just hope and pray that the little children of the world never hear you saying a thing like that about Eaton's. Now don't try to weasel out, Santa, I heard you say it. You're lying! You did not say, "Up *Prancer*." Pardon? You're going to *what* this Christmas? Well, that's just about the last straw. I never would have believed you'd stoop that low. *(Phone is slammed down.)*

SR. EXEC: He's not coming to our store?

JR. EXEC: Worse than that, R.J. He's threatening to tell all the little kids there's no such place as Eaton's . . . that it's really Simpson's!

AS THE TWIG IS BENT

Dr. Samuel Laycock, prominent Canadian educator and authority on gifted children, believes and has stated publicly that the gifted child is far less likely to become a delinquent than the dull child.

A typical Canadian kitchen. The wife is at the stove. The husband is seated at the table waiting for the meal to be served.

WIFE: We'll eat in about five minutes, dear. Just waiting for the vegetables to do. *(Phone rings . . . Wife answers.)* Hello? Yes it is . . . Oh, dear! Are you quite sure, sergeant? Well, thank you for calling. We'll certainly do what we can. *(Puts phone down.)* That was the Youth Bureau of the Metropolitan Police. They caught Derwent redhanded this afternoon stealing bicycles.

HUSBAND: What? Not our Derwent! It's gotta be a mistake.

WIFE: The sergeant was very nice. Said they gave him a warning and are sending him home with the understanding that we'd talk to him about his delinquency.

HUSBAND *(Pounding his fist into his hand)*: Who can you trust? I ask you . . . *Who* can you trust! These so-called experts . . . these know-it-all child psychologists . . . they're always saying a gifted child won't become a delinquent and we believed 'em. We thought we were secure in the knowledge that Derwent is a gifted child. Wouldn't you say Derwent was a gifted child?

WIFE: Yes, I certainly would.

[*A car screeches to a stop in the drive. Kitchen door flies open.*]

DERWENT: D'uh, hi gang!

HUSBAND: Well, I just hope you're proud of yourself son. You sure let us down real good. We've always believed that gifted children wouldn't become delinquents and you're gifted, Derwent. God knows you're gifted. Can you think of any kid on the block who's more gifted than you?

DERWENT: D'uh, I guess not.

HUSBAND: I mean your I.Q. may be only 65 but, boy, you're gifted. And I'm gonna change that right now!

DERWENT: D'uh, you mean you're gonna raise my I.Q.?

HUSBAND: No, stoopid! I'm takin' back the gifts . . . starting with the convertible, the $50 a week allowance, that key to the Playboy Club and the seat on the Toronto stock exchange.

YOU TELL ME YOUR BILL — I'LL TELL YOU MINE

The Speaker of the House has often complained that Parliament gets bogged down with private members' bills. These range in scope from proposals to salute Little League Baseball to the regulating and licensing of rain-making equipment in Canada. The House generally sets aside an hour each day to debate these grabbers. One member, alone, sponsored forty such bills during the past session.

THE SCENE:

A typical day in the House of Commons.

MEMBER: Now my next bill deals with something that I feel is a downright disgrace and I'd just like to get the opinion of some of the Honourable members on it. I have it right here. It's from Quong Lee's Hand Laundry back in my home riding and it's for $5.75. Now believe it or not, that's just for three white shirts I left in and I didn't even ask for starch. . . . (*Desk thumping and cries of "shame" from government benches.*) All right . . . all right . . . I see you guys aren't too concerned about the cost of living these days in this land of ours. I'll move on and introduce my next bill. He's up there in the Public Gallery just behind the lady in the flowered hat. It's his first visit to

Ottawa. Bill, will you stand up so the folks can see you? Bill McGoon, gang. One heck of a nice guy . . . past president of our Rotary . . . three times Yo-Yo champ of Manitoba. What's say we give him a real warm . . . *(More thumping and angry shouts from government benches.)* Geez, you guys sure know how to roll out the old welcome mat. O.K., moving along now I'd like to present another bill . . . one that's been sort of a special favourite of mine for quite a few years. I was hoping to present this one with a little panache . . . sort of dress it up a little . . . but when I asked George Hees to play piano for me he turned me down flat. A real prince. Anyways, gang, here's the bill I had in mind and I sure hope you like it.

He's just my Bill
An ordinary guy
You'd pass him on the street
And never notice. . . .

(Violent desk thumping . . . cries of "shame" . . . cascades of spitballs from government benches.) Aw, come on you guys. Give me a chance, will ya? Geez, you sure stand four square behind the little guy, don't ya! What is this . . . a police state? Is there no place in our way of life for the private member's bill. Must it always be power politics? Now, come on you guys.

CHACUN A SON GOUT

When Unionville, Ontario, opened its new home for senior citizens about a year ago a lot of eyebrows were raised at the large metal sculpture which dominated the front lawn. It depicted a nude man playfully tossing his grandchild into the air above his head. The anatomical detail of the sculpture gave rise to charges of obscenity.

THE SCENE:

The front lawn of the senior citizens' home. Birds chirping, old folks wandering about and, by the statue, CBC reporter Leslie Lovelace, tastefully and tactfully conducting an opinion poll.

LOVELACE: Good afternoon, Canada, from the lovely lawn in front of Union Villa, a new concept in homes for Senior Citizens. Immediately behind me is the controversial sculpture which a lot of people are calling obscene. But in spite of the criticism, Federal Housing Minister, Robert Andras, has said; "We intend to provide more homes like this in the future, homes which give the residents a total environment where all their needs can be taken care of." With me at my CBC microphone is Geoffery Wheeler. He's eighty-three and a resident of the home. Mr. Wheeler, what is your opinion of the statue?

WHEELER: Well, sir. I go along with the housing minister. As long as this here statue is functional and satisfies our needs I'm all for it. All I know is it comes in damn handy on a hot day when you peel off your vest and coat and are lookin' for some place to hang em. I just take the coat and vest and I hang em . . . right about here. . . .

LOVELACE: Well . . . uh . . . yes . . . I see . . . uh . . . Madam! Would you care to express your opinion of this statue?

OLD LADY: Well, mercy, I just think it's great. It certainly solved my problem.

LOVELACE (*Apprehensively*): Your . . . your problem?

OLD LADY: Yes. I always come out here in the winter time with a few crusts of bread for the birds. But when I toss the bread out it sinks down in the deep snow and the poor birds can't find it. Now, all I have to do is brush the snow off . . . right about here . . . set all the little pieces of bread on here . . . all in a row . . . and we've got a dandy

feeding station. I'm so pleased they went and built a real big statue. There's room for about forty starlings to perch along here . . . won't have to be peckin' at each other for standin' room.

LOVELACE: Well, thank you madam. I was hoping, actually, to deal with the aesthetic rather than the functional merits of the sculpture. Perhaps this gentleman here would care to express an opinion in that area.

VERY OLD MAN: I'm not expressin' no opinions on nuthin'.

LOVELACE: I'm sorry sir. I noticed you standing here these past few minutes and I just thought you were waiting for a chance to say something.

VERY OLD MAN: I'm waitin' fer you to move to one side and clear the front of that there statue so's I can get a clear swing at 'er.

LOVELACE: A clear swing at the statue?

VERY OLD MAN: 'Course. The only way a body can punch open a tin of pop around this place. Kitchen staff never seem to have no punches around so I jest bring my tin of pop out here, haul off and give it a good swing against the statue . . . right bout here.

[*Sound of the metallic crunch of a tin being punctured.*]

OLD LADY: Gracious!!! I just hope you never do that when the little birds are sitting there . . . poor little things would die of fright.

OLD MAN: And ya better not try that when my coat's hangin' there cause if that pop spews over my coat you'll git five gnarled knuckles right in the mouth.

VERY OLD MAN: I got as much right to open my tin of pop on that statue as you have to hang your stoopid coat on it.

OLD LADY: I think you're both selfish brutes. Give me starlings any day.

BOTH MEN: Now you just stay out of it, ya hear.

OLD LADY: Don't you raise your voices at me or I'll jab a hat pin up your left nostril.

LOVELACE: (*Striving to be heard over the developing Donnybrook*): This is Leslie Lovelace returning you to our studios.

Following the sale to an American company last year of Canada's major text book publishers, the 140-year-old Ryerson Press, it seems safe to assume that future generations of Canadian students should graduate without any jingoistic or chauvinistic delusions about their national heritage.

THE SCENE:

A Canadian classroom.

TEACHER: Quiet, children, please! Now I know you're all very excited over these new text books we've just received but let's simmer down and we'll all take our first look at these handsome, new books which we'll be using for the first time this year. This one here is entitled *A Child's Garden of Canadian Verse* and right here on page one we find a delightful poem called: "The Song My Paddle Sings."

PUPIL: But teacher, we already took that last year . . . it's by Pauline Johnson.

TEACHER: No, no, dear. Not this one. This is by the famous American, Al Capp, and it's all about how a teacher instils the right ideas into the minds of young people by use of corporal punishment.

PUPIL: Gee, whizz. Isn't Pauline Johnson in that book?

TEACHER: Well, now, let's just browze through it and find out. Oh yes, here we are. "Pauline Johnson. An Indian poetess chiefly remembered for two things . . . her great-grandson Lyndon who became president of the United States and her great-nephew, Jack, who became one of America's first heavy-weight boxing champions. Now, children, I'd like to turn for a moment to our new history text. It has the lovely title *The Romance of Canada*. As you can see, it's just loaded with lovely, coloured pictures of the great events in our history. Look! Here's one showing the famous Battle of Queenston Heights with the American soldiers driving the Canadians and the British regulars helter-skelter into the Niagara River.

PUPIL: Golly, teacher, I always thought Canada won that battle.

TEACHER: No, dear. You must be thinking about the old text we used last year. This new publisher can afford much better research techniques and a higher level of scholarship.

PUPIL: Well, is General Brock in that picture?

TEACHER: That's strange he doesn't seem to be. It lists the names of all the important men taking part but I don't see . . . oh, wait a minute. It says here . . . "Absent when the picture was taken is General Brock who got drunk before the battle, climbed to the top of the Brock monument and attempted to show off in front of his troops by standing on his head. He fell off and fractured his skull."

PUPIL: Teacher! What about the Battle of Lundy's Lane. Is that in there?

TEACHER: Lundy's Lane. I'll check it dear . . . just a moment . . . Lane . . . Lane . . . Ah, here we are, Lane. No, it doesn't seem to be listed . . . let's see there's Frankie . . . Lois (*see* Superman) . . . no, I guess it isn't here. Well, let's move on to our new text in mathematics. That's one subject that never varies. The cold, unswerving, objective truth of math, unlike history or literature, always manages to withstand the blowing winds of change. Now, if you'll all have your pencils and paper ready I'll just read out a typical problem that youngsters your age have wrestled with for generations. Let's see, now. How about this one on the top of page three: "In the Vietnamese village of My Lai there are 387 people. If a U.S. marine lieutenant kills 180, how many will be left to cheer the liberation of their village from the brutality of the Viet Cong?"

JUST TELL EM RON SENT YOU

A new era seems to have dawned for the Canadian consumer. Thanks to the tireless efforts of Consumer Affairs Minister, Ron Basford, manufacturers are now required to state on their cans and cartons just what's inside and how much of it. The name and address of the manufacturer must also appear on the labelling to enable consumers to track him down when they wish to lodge a complaint.

THE SCENE:

A lovely, sheltered valley filled with bird-song and the laughter of little brooks. Along one of the footpaths, a figure approaches. He is angry . . . he is a consumer.

IRATE CONSUMER (*Out of breath*): So there you are! I've finally tracked you down! Well, it's taken me a long time but boy it's gonna be worth it. I'm gonna clean your clock and clean it good! I bought one of your tins, fella, that said "Net Weight 12 oz." on the label but when I weighed the contents they were only 11.8 ounces. So I took your name off the label and I'm gonna give you five right in the mouth. And that's only the beginning, cause when *I* get through with you, Ron Basford's gonna take over and believe me, fella, there's one guy that can put the fear of . . . AAAAAAAAAAHHHHHHHHHHHH!!!!!
[*A sickening crunch as of human bones fragmenting.*]
TINY VOICE: Gee, you squashed him with your little finger!
[*Deafening roar: Ho, Ho, Ho . . . Ron Basford.*]
TINY VOICE: Golly . . . Green Giant!
[*Deafening roar: Ho, Ho, Ho . . . Ron Basford.*]

THERE HE GOES — OUR PRIME MINISTER

Among all the accolades bestowed on our Prime Minister, perhaps the most flattering was to have his name included by a London tabloid, The Daily Sketch, *among its list of the world's ten sexiest men. Mr. Trudeau was ranked seventh among the men "who, more than any others, set female hearts the world over, beating ever faster."*

THE SCENE:

Late evening on a residential street in Ottawa. The sound of light traffic is almost totally submerged by the predominance of female sighs and the thumping of an aroused heart.

TRUDEAU: Well, here we are at your front door. It's been a most enjoyable evening and I do hope you'll consent to go out with me again in the not too distant future. (*The sighs and heartbeats have grown too loud to ignore.*) Really, I must say I find this rather awkward and embarrassing. I have no idea why you should be reacting in this manner. I'm just an ordinary human being . . . true, nature has been kind to me but I certainly don't go out of my way to cultivate this irresistible quality. I mean, just because Woman's Day used me as their centrefold this month, surely that's no reason for you to lose all emotional control like this. Surely there must be some explanation.

FEMALE: Yes . . . there . . . is . . . I . . . thought . . . you would have . . . guessed . . . already. It's because . . . well . . . it's because . . . I'm a woman . . . with all the . . . weaknesses . . . of my sex. There's nothing . . . I can do . . . about it. . . . There's no point trying to . . . to fight it. No matter . . . how hard I try . . . I just can NOT jog 35 miles without . . . getting . . . winded.

TRUDEAU: Well, of course, it wasn't my fault that the Mercedes happened to break down in the Gatineau Hills. I suppose I could have called a taxi but it seemed such a lovely evening and jogging is such a great conditioner . . . and besides that, a penny saved is a penny earned. The fact that you're in poor physical condition is really no fault of mine. I happen to have a black belt in Judo, I ski faster than a speeding bullet and if it weren't for wet blankets like Stanfield, I'm quite sure I could leap over the House of Commons in a single bound.

ONE OF THE OLD SCHOOL

An eminent British surgeon, Thomas Stowell, claims to know the true identity of the infamous London murderer, Jack the Ripper. Though refusing to divulge the name for fear of "doing harm to a family I love and respect," Dr. Stowell has managed to drop enough innuendos to leave little doubt that he feels the culprit was the Duke of Clarence, older brother of George V.

A BBC London studio. Young announcer, Osmond Dwight-Frisby, interviews Dr. Stowell.

FRISBY: Dr. Stowell, the BBC and, indeed, the British public are most anxious to get to the bottom of this controversy to which your unusual speculations have given rise. From the clues which you've given publicly, the *Sunday Times* has already suggested that Jack the Ripper was, in fact, Victoria's grandson . . . elder brother of George V. Would you be willing to corroborate this?

STOWELL: No, no, no, no . . . no point whatsoever in trying to pump me, young man. I've already made it quite clear I have no desire to harm a family which I love and respect. Besides, if I were to give you his name it certainly wouldn't end there. I know you chaps. You wouldn't rest until you'd also wheedled and pried out of me the true identity of the master-mind behind the Great Train Robbery of a few years ago.

FRISBY: You . . . you also know that man's identity!

STOWELL: Of course I do. But it won't do you any good to try to pry it out of me. I have far too much love and respect for his family. I know full well how little regard you chaps in this news business have for personal feelings but I'd rather die than embarrass the innocent members of his family. I certainly will not give the Welsh people the opportunity of publicly stoning this man's son whenever he might go there on state occasions. Nor will I allow a cruel and fickle public to demand the removal of his wife's image from all our coins and stamps.

FRISBY: Then you flatly refuse to divulge this man's identity.

STOWELL: Most assuredly!! I realize fair play is no longer fashionable but, by Jove, there are a few of us left who have some semblance of old fashioned decency. Try as you may, sir, you'll not get the name out of me!

A BBC London studio. Young announcer, Osmond Dwight-Frisby, interviews Dr. Stowell.

FRISBY: Dr. Stowell, the BBC and, indeed, the British public are most anxious to get to the bottom of this controversy to which your unusual speculations have given rise. From the clues which you've given publicly, the *Sunday Times* has already suggested that Jack the Ripper was, in fact, Victoria's grandson . . . elder brother of George V. Would you be willing to corroborate this?

STOWELL: No, no, no, no . . . no point whatsoever in trying to pump me, young man. I've already made it quite clear I have no desire to harm a family which I love and respect. Besides, if I were to give you his name it certainly wouldn't end there. I know you chaps. You wouldn't rest until you'd also wheedled and pried out of me the true identity of the master-mind behind the Great Train Robbery of a few years ago.

FRISBY: You . . . you also know that man's identity!

STOWELL: Of course I do. But it won't do you any good to try to pry it out of me. I have far too much love and respect for his family. I know full well how little regard you chaps in this news business have for personal feelings but I'd rather die than embarrass the innocent members of his family. I certainly will not give the Welsh people the opportunity of publicly stoning this man's son whenever he might go there on state occasions. Nor will I allow a cruel and fickle public to demand the removal of his wife's image from all our coins and stamps.

FRISBY: Then you flatly refuse to divulge this man's identity.

STOWELL: Most assuredly!! I realize fair play is no longer fashionable but, by Jove, there are a few of us left who have some semblance of old fashioned decency. Try as you may, sir, you'll not get the name out of me!

Certainly, the two most bizarre news stories of the past year or so were, first, the report from England that Jack the Ripper might well have been the Duke of Clarence, grandson of Queen Victoria. This was closely followed by the claim of two U.S. air force officers that the renowned American flyer, Amelia Earhart, really hadn't died in a South Pacific plane crash in 1937. According to their research, she was living under an assumed name in New Jersey, having spent World War Two in Emperor Hirohito's palace. One didn't quite know what to expect next.

THE SCENE:

A noisy hallway in the West Block of the Parliament Buildings jammed with the excited reporters of all the news media.

COLLISTER: This is Ron Collister speaking from Ottawa. Well, the shock waves from the bombshell dropped by the news media on an unsuspecting nation late yesterday are still reverberating through the corridors and offices of Parliament Hill. At the moment, I'm fighting my way through a densely packed crowd of newsmen toward Mr. Stanfield who is about ten feet away and in just a few moments I hope to be able to pick up on our CBC microphone the first public statement which he has consented to make since that first news bulletin began rocking an astounded Canadian public yesterday.

STANFIELD: Uh . . . I . . . uh . . . I would just like to say to every Canadian . . . uh . . . that I'm very sorry about . . . uh . . . about this whole affair. I mean . . . uh . . . I never really dreamed that the story would leak out . . . uh . . . especially after all these years. But, uh . . . now that it has . . . uh

. . . let me say this. Uh . . . to err is human . . . uh . . . to forgive divine . . . uh.

COLLISTER: Mr. Stanfield, can you recreate for us the turbulent chain of events as you recall them from that fateful day?

STANFIELD: Uh . . . well . . . yes. I . . . uh . . . I believe I can. As I recall that day . . . uh . . . there was a lot of panic . . . uh . . . a lot of confusion. Buildings were collapsing . . . uh . . . bullets flying everywhere. Shells were falling and . . . uh . . . quite a few fires had broken out. I was just sitting there . . . uh . . . feeling pretty rotten . . . I mean I could see all my dreams collapsing around me so . . . uh . . . I . . . I took this cyanide pill out of my pocket. But . . . uh . . . before I could pop it into my mouth . . . why . . . uh . . . Eva . . . or Miss Braun I guess I should say . . . uh . . . she gave me this banana instead and she said . . . uh . . . she said . . . look, why don't you shave off that crazy little moustache . . . uh . . . comb that hair out of your eyes and see if you can't make it to some place like . . . uh . . . well . . . like South America or Canada . . . start all over again in politics. After all . . . uh . . . she argued . . . uh . . . you're forceful and . . . uh . . . dynamic . . . uh . . . and . . . uh . . . you . . . uh . . . you're . . . uh . . . you're still the same old spellbinder . . . uh . . . when it comes to . . . uh . . . to public speaking. Well, it seemed . . . uh . . . kind of a wild idea . . . but . . . uh . . . anyway I said owweederzeen to Eva and . . . uh . . . I started crawling out of the . . . uh . . . bunker . . . you see . . . uh . . . and. . . .

[*The voice trails off, drowned out by an avalanche of reporters racing to phone their papers.*]

CAN YOU TELL ME THE COST OF THE
BONAVENTURE REFIT?

I wonder just how many Canadians are availing themselves of the learning opportunities provided by Information Canada? After all, they're the ones who are financing this rather expensive exercise in participatory democracy. If you have any question concerning this great land of ours, the answer is as close as your telephone.

THE SCENE:

The electronic nerve-centre of Information Canada in Ottawa.

[*Phone rings and is picked up.*]

OFFICIAL (*Breezily*): Hell-o! Information Liberal . . . uh . . . no, no . . . I'm sorry . . . as you were . . . Hell-o! Information Canada!

CHILD: Um . . . uh . . . mister?

OFFICIAL: Yes, sonny?

CHILD: Like, I'm doing a project in our Current Affairs course at school. And . . . um . . . I would like to find out what the government is doing to help the Indians.

OFFICIAL: Just one moment son. I'll just flip through my card catalogue index here and we'll have it for you in a jiffy . . . let's see now . . . India Rubber Ball . . . Indian Arm Wrestling . . . Indian Leg Wrestling . . . Indianapolis Speedway . . . Indian Problem . . . ah, here we are! Are you all set, son?

CHILD: Yes, sir.

OFFICIAL (*Reading*): The Federal Government, through the smoothly oiled machinery of the Department of Indian Affairs, has pledged an unrelenting effort to alleviate the distress of Canadian Indians to the end that they, along with their white brothers, may fully enjoy all the advantages of our Canadian way of life as laid down by the Canadian Bill of Rights. And now, this is Information Canada thanking you for calling and reminding you to keep those cards and letters coming in.

CHILD: No, no! Wait! Wait! Gee, mister, I wanted to find out about things like what kind of jobs Indians can get and, um . . . like, what kind of houses they have to live in and . . . um . . . what happens to them like when the government out in British Columbia floods all their land to make those big hydro dams . . . you know, things like that.

OFFICIAL: Well, son, I think you can appreciate the vast number of calls we have to answer each day on an infinite variety of subjects. That's why we, the men who man the phones here, can only give you a cursory or generalized summation. We do, however, provide you with a reference listing . . . a sort of bibliography . . . if you know what that means, son.

CHILD: Like the names of a whole lot of books?

OFFICIAL: Right, son. A carefully chosen list of suggested reading material which will guide you helpfully through your area of interest, enabling you to discover in detail the answer to your specific query. Now have you got your pencil and paper ready?

CHILD: Yep.

OFFICIAL: Here we go, son. The . . . Song . . . My . . . Paddle . . . Sings . . . by Pauline Johnson.

CHILD (*With obedient trust*): The . . . Song . . . My . . . Paddle . . . Sings . . . by Pauline. . . .

OFFICIAL: Indian . . . Love . . . Call . . . by Rudolph Friml.

CHILD: Indian . . . Love . . . Call . . . by Rud. . . .

OFFICIAL: Oh . . . the . . . Moon . . . Shines . . . Tonight . . . on . . . Pretty . . . Redwing . . . lyrics by J. W. Primrose . . . music by A. R. Montague.

CHILD: Oh . . . The . . . (*The phone is hung up.*) Hello? Hello? Mister? . . . Hello?

GOD BLESS U.S., HENRY FORD

About a year ago, when the membership of the United Auto Workers accepted a settlement offer from Ford Motor Company in Detroit, they were guaranteed, among other benefits, that each worker would receive a Christmas bonus of $175. I couldn't help thinking what a far cry from Dickens' Christmas Carol *and Bob Cratchett's big bonus — the day off and a goose.*

THE SCENE:

The modest home of a Ford worker on Christmas Eve.

MOTHER: Well, Tim, it's Christmas Eve and your father will soon be home but I just don't know what Christmas holds in store for us this year.

TIM: Why, mommy?

MOTHER: Well, son, your father has to work for these mean, penny-pinching men. I dropped over to the plant to take his lunch to him today and there he was, the poor man, sitting blowing on his hands.

TIM: Don't the mean men heat the building, mommy?

MOTHER: Well, yes, son. But to make ends meet your father has to spend his lunch hour shooting crap and for some reason he feels he can do better if he blows on his hands before each throw.

TIM: Will daddy get Christmas off, mommy?

MOTHER: Oh yes. They give him a few days at Christmas and at New Year's but, of course, to make up for it he'll have to work on Bastille Day and Pancake Tuesday. You can't squeeze blood from a stone, son.

TIM: Someday, mommy, if daddy gets a raise will I still have to hobble around on these old wooden things.

MOTHER: I certainly hope not, son. (*The front door opens.*) Oh, that must be your father now.

TIM: I'm going to meet him . . . I'm going to meet him. . . .

MOTHER: Careful son . . . don't fall!

FATHER: I'm home, Martha. Come on Tim . . . if you can walk this far without falling, your old dad will let you sit up on his shoulders.

MOTHER: How did things go, Bob?

FATHER: We got it, Martha! One hundred and seventy-five bucks!

TIM: Daddy, daddy . . . does that mean? . . . does that really mean?

FATHER: That's right son. Your mother and I won't have to watch you struggling with those things anymore. Here, hold onto daddy's neck for a minute.

TIM: What are you going to do?

FATHER: You're finished having to use these darn things, Tim. I'm getting rid of them once and for all.

[*The sound of the smashing of wood is heard.*]

TIM: But, golly, dad . . . they're the only skis I've got!

FATHER: Not any more son. I'm getting you the best pair of fibreglass, triple-flex, steel-edge competition skis that money can buy . . . with Jean Claude Killy written all over em! And what's more, we're all spending Christmas in Sun Valley!

TIM: God bless us, everyone!

PLEASE FASTEN YOUR DIAPERS

Women whose jobs fall under the jurisdiction of the Federal Government are going to be entitled to a minimum of twelve weeks maternity leave in the event of pregnancy. In some medical quarters this period is still not considered sufficient.

THE SCENE:

A private room on the maternity floor of a large hospital

[*The door opens.*]

DOCTOR: Well, well, well . . . and how are we this morning?

WOMAN: Oh, just great doctor. Look! The nurse just brought him in for his first feeding. I'm so excited!

DOCTOR: Yes, that' a fine, healthy baby. Are you pleased it's a boy?

WOMAN: Well, with the first I don't really care whether the engine is inboard or outboard.

DOCTOR: Uh . . . yes. You're a stewardess with Air Canada, I understand.

WOMAN: Yes, I am.

DOCTOR: Tell me, how do you feel about this twelve-week maternity leave?

WOMAN: Oh, I think it's going to be a great help, doctor.

DOCTOR: Well, there are two schools of thought on the subject. Some of us on staff here at the hospital feel it's not nearly long enough. I mean a young girl spends months, even years, learning a profession, developing special skills, acquiring special knowledge in order to do a good job. Then, suddenly, she becomes pregnant and faces perhaps the most important job of all . . . motherhood. And yet she's given only twelve weeks to prepare for that job.

WOMAN: Well, of course, doctor I can't speak for girls in

other professions but I think I've been very fortunate working as a stewardess these past eight years with Air Canada. I regard this precious little bundle here as ... well ... as a little first-class passenger and it's my job to welcome him aboard and make him as comfortable as possible. It comes so naturally ... it's ... well it's almost an instinct with me because of my Air Canada training. So, you see, in my case these twelve weeks maternity leave are more than enough.

DOCTOR: Well, I'm delighted to hear that. Now, I'd better clear out of here and let you get on with that important job of motherhood.

WOMAN: Thanks for dropping by, doctor. (*Door opens and closes. Baby begins to gurgle and coo.*) Now then, how's our little passenger doing? We'll just fluff that pillow up ... and make sure that your head is in the upright position ... all righty? Now then ... tea, coffee or milk? (*Baby cries.*) Tea, coffee or milk? (*Cries get more insistent.*) Sweetheart, mommy doesn't know unless you tell her ... tea, coffee or milk? (*As the cries grow louder the Air Canada aplomb disintegrates.*) What's wrong? Can I get you a magazine? What's wrong? Tell mommy. That's what I'm here for. Do you want a lifesaver? ... something from the bar? ... oh, dear, what'll I do? ... what'll I do! ! ! !

GORILLA TACTICS

In December. 1970, the last anti-evolution law was finally repealed in the United States. In the state of Mississippi, it is no longer a criminal offence to teach that man has descended from a lower order of animals.

In the sultry summer heat of a small Mississippi town two men lounge against the wall outside the sheriff's office.

SHERIFF: You know, Bull, it's kinda depressin' the way this hyah state o' Miss'ssipi (*Ejects a jet of tobacco juice*) has slowly gone downhill.

BULL: Ah know jest what ya mean, sheriff. All them little things that made up a way o' life that decent, law-abidin' folk could cling to have gradjlly been chipped away.

SHERIFF: Ah mind all the good-natured fun and laughs Ah used to be able to git on school openin' day, roughin' up them niggrah kids whilst they waited fer that white kindergarten to open. (*More tobacco juice hits the dirt.*)

BULL: Yeah . . . nowadays if ya as much as throw one teensy-weensy bomb into a niggrah Sunday School class there's bound to be somebody gonna raise a eyebrow.

SHERIFF: Folks is gettin' their heads filled with all kinds of crazy ideas. You cain't even fire off a twelve-gauge shotgun into a carful of them commie civil-rights trash without gittin' a suspended sentence.

BULL: Well, reckon that's what happens when ya git a federal government crawlin' with commies and Jews.

SHERIFF: Tell ya one thing, Bull. They cain't sink much lower into moral turpitood and godless immorality when they make it legal for to teach our young uns that we are *not* made in God's image . . . that we's descended from a lower order of animals.

BULL: It sure as hell makes a holla mockery outta the nobility of man (*The tobacco juice doesn't quite clear his boot.*) and all them other Christian values white folks cherish and hold dear.

I wonder whatever became of Captain Susan R. Struck? She's the unwed U.S. air force officer who had a baby while still in the service and then lost an appeal to be allowed to remain with the air force. A U.S. appeals court upheld the air force decision to discharge any woman officer who becomes pregnant.

[*Sound of the soothing creak of a rocker moving to and fro.*]

MOTHER: My, it's real nice to have you home again, Susan. You gonna be staying for a while this time?

SUSAN: I guess so, mother.

MOTHER: What? You'll have to speak up dear.

SUSAN: I said I guess so, mother.

MOTHER: Well, what better place to come to, child, when you're feeling blue and need some cheering up. That's what a mother's for . . . to give comfort and understanding. You certainly didn't get much from your friends in the air force . . . comfort I mean.

SUSAN: I just wish I hadn't lost my appeal.

MOTHER: What, dear?

SUSAN (*a little edgy*): I said, mother, I just wish I hadn't lost my appeal.

MOTHER: Well, I wish you'd lost it about nine months ago dear. A plain girl doesn't get into trouble. You show me a girl with lots of appeal, and I'll show you. . . .

SUSAN: Oh, mother! Please! I just never dreamed they'd kick me out. I was sure I'd just get a reprimand and perhaps reduced to the ranks or. . . .

MOTHER: Seduced by the ranks! Land sakes, child, isn't one enough?

SUSAN: Mother, will you please listen! I said . . . reduced . . . to . . . the . . . ranks.

MOTHER: Oh.

SUSAN: They didn't have to kick me out. It would have been quite enough just to parade me before the C.O. and rip off my pips.

MOTHER: Oh, Susan, they wouldn't dare! Not to a nursing mother! Surely! The more I hear of the U.S. air force, the less I like it. Bunch of sadistic brutes. Yes, dear, I think you're much better off back home with an understanding mother.

OF THINGS TO COME

There have been many strange and unusual Santa Claus stories in the papers over the years. I wonder how long it will be before we see this one?

THE SCENE:

Christmas Eve outside Santa's workshop. The sleigh stands loaded and waiting.

MRS. CLAUS: Now let's just check it once again, Fat, to make sure everything's on there.

SANTA: Oh, ho, ho . . . everything's there, my dear.

MRS. CLAUS: Are the reindeer all hitched to the sleigh?

SANTA: Bless my soul, yes. They're all ready to go. Oh, ho, ho, ho.

MRS. CLAUS: What about Rudolph's nose. Have you got it painted red in case of fog?

SANTA: Oh, ho, ho . . . yes, of course. I wouldn't forget a thing like that.

MRS. CLAUS: Did you check the list? Are you sure you've got all the kiddies' names down there?

SANTA: Nothing to worry about, my dear. They're all there. Oh, ho, ho, ho.

MRS. CLAUS: Well, I guess everything's all set. Now give me a kiss and we'll see you in the morning.

[*Sound of the smack of a kiss.*]

SANTA: Good-bye, my dear.

MRS. CLAUS: Good-bye, Santa.

SANTA: Oh, ho, ho, ho, ho, ho, ho. . . .

MRS. CLAUS: And for heaven's sake don't stand outside in your underwear all night Oh-ho-ho-ing. There's a sink full of dirty dishes inside and the workshop's a mess. Up prancer . . . up Dancer . . . up Betty Friedan . . . up Anne Francis . . . up Simone de Beauvoir . . . we're away . . . oh, tee, hee, hee, hee, hee.

IL Y AURA TOUJOURS UN ANGLETERRE

Consumer Affairs Minister Ronald Basford has pledged that by 1975 bilingual labelling on all consumer goods will be mandatory, even in Victoria, B.C.

THE SCENE:

An elderly, British gentleman approaches the front door of his rose-covered, red-white-and-blue cottage on a quiet residential street in Victoria.

CEDRIC (*singing to himself*): Land of hope and glory . . . mother of the free. . . . (*Door opens and closes.*) Agatha! Agatha! I'm home my dear.

AGATHA: Oh, good show, Cedric. That didn't take you long. Did you get everything?

[*Sound of the rustle of parcels coming out of a shopping bag.*]

CEDRIC: Everything, my dear . . . plus this little bargain I came across quite by chance. Anthology of French poems for only seventy cents, by Jove. Oh, by the way, I shouldn't leave this lying about if I were you. You know what these French poets are like. However, it's a rattling good bargain . . . even if the title does sound a bit earthy.

AGATHA: Cedric, "pommes de terre" does *not* mean earthy poems. This is a bag of potatoes.

CEDRIC: Oh, blast! You know it did feel a bit lumpy for an anthology.

AGATHA: Did you get my deordorant, dear?

CEDRIC: Oh, yes. Mind you I had a devil of a time. So many commercial brands on the market, you know. Couldn't remember for the life of me whether you used Calm or Poise.

AGATHA: I use Calm, dear.

CEDRIC: Oh bad show. Dreadfully sorry . . . I'm afraid I bought you Poise.

AGATHA: Quite all right, dear. They're all about the same . . . Cedric!

CEDRIC: Yes, me dear?

AGATHA: This seems to be a tin of garden peas.

CEDRIC: What? But surely, my dear, Poise is a ladies' deodorant!

AGATHA: Not when it's spelled P-O-I-S, Cedric. That's French, dear. Pronounced "pwaw."

CEDRIC: Oh, blast!

AGATHA: What's in that tube there?

CEDRIC: This? Oh, it's one of those auto repair kits. I'm sick and tired of paying the garage a king's ransom everytime I get a tiny dent in the car. With this, you simply fill in the crevices, wait till it hardens and then paint over it.

AGATHA: It says here on the tube it contains fluoride. Why do you suppose they'd put fluoride in plastic cement dear?

CEDRIC: Ours not to reason why, my dear. But I'm quite sure that when the manufacturers say "Pour les dents" they know what they're talking about, what?

AGATHA: Oh, Cedric!

CEDRIC: Eh? What?

AGATHA: It's tooth-paste! You've bought a tube of tooth-paste!

CEDRIC: Blast, blast blast! ! Why does that vulgar Ronald Basford have to muck about with our commercial labels! Keep Canada British, I say. That stupid Basford.

AGATHA: Really, dear, there's no need to be foul-mouthed.

CEDRIC: Rule Britannia . . . Britannia rules the waves . . . Britons never, never, never. . . .

ON YOUR WRIST AS IN THE HOUSE — FAITHFUL FOREVER

Last Christmas, the Trudeau wrist-watch made its first appearance in Montreal stores. Bearing a photo of the Prime Minister on the face, the $14.95 Swiss-made watch has red hands and a red maple leaf at each quarter hour. It could well become as much a part of our Canadian Christmas as mistletoe and plum pudding.

THE SCENE:

Christmas morning in a Saskatchewan farm home.

MARTHA: I don't care how much ya paid for it, Alvin, it's not what I wanted for Christmas.

ALVIN: But Martha . . . just look at how nice it fills that empty corner of the parlour.

MARTHA: I asked for a Trudeau wrist-watch.

ALVIN: Martha, that cabinet is made outta solid English oak!

MARTHA: I wanted a Trudeau wrist-watch.

ALVIN: Martha, be reasonable! That pendulum is solid brass!

MARTHA: You can just take it back where you got it, Alvin.

ALVIN: Martha, just give the thing a chance. Here! Let me push the hands to the nearest hour agin.

MARTHA: You can push the whole shebang to the nearest junk-yard.

ALVIN: Hush up, Martha. I'm gonna set it at three o'clock.

[*Sound of chimes, then interior mechanical activity.*]

Lookit, Martha! Lookit! Here he comes.

DIEFENBAKER VOICE: Cuckoo . . . uh . . . cuckoo . . . uh . . . cuckoo. Uh, it is now . . . uh, more or less . . . three o'clock.

ALVIN: Let's see your Trudeau wrist-watch do that!

MARTHA: I told you . . . I wanted a Trudeau wrist-watch.

ALVIN: Sssshhhh! Martha! It's bi-lingewal!

DIEFENBAKER VOICE: Cuckoo . . . uh, cuckoo . . . uh, cuckoo. Eeel est, mayntenant, troys oors.

MARTHA: Lookit, Alvin. I don't care if he recites the Canadian Bill of Rights in Mandarin Chinese. I want a Trudeau wrist-watch. You've ruined my whole Christmas . . . ruined it, do ya hear, ruined it!

THIS ABOVE ALL

Fortunately, one of the shortest-lived innovations in the field of education was the attempt early this year of the Canadian Liberal University Students Association to set up a free essay bank. It was an attempt to counteract the high cost of cheating by enabling the

young leaders of tomorrow to simply pick up some-
one else's essay, lie to their professors that it was
their own, and thus save time which could be spent
on campus political involvement.

THE SCENE:

A boisterous student political meeting. The rap of a
gavel calls for order.

TOMORROW'S YOUNG HOPE: Uh, gang, could you all just simmer
down please? If I could have your attention, I'd like to get
this meeting underway. I think all of us present here this
evening owe a real debt of gratitude to those hard-working association members who set up the free essay bank.
Not only have they made it possible for us to pick up an
A-plus without any sweat but they're also responsible for
our being here tonight instead of trying to grind out some
stupid essay. So what do you say, gang, in keeping with
the decent Christian tradition of this great country of
ours, what do you say we all bow our heads for a few
seconds and each in his own way, ask divine blessing for
those essay bank organizers. (*A five second pause*) Now,
gang, I know we're all real pleased to be able to use this
Convocation Hall as our meeting place this week. It sure
beats that dumpy old boiler room down in the Field House.
For this, I think we all owe a vote of thanks to a real hustl-
ing, go-getting young Liberal . . . Arnold Underhand.
Arnie got into the president's office this week, under the
pretext of discussing his courses, and while the old goat
wasn't looking, Arnie slipped his hand into the desk
drawer and stole the key to Convocation Hall. How about
that? Let's hear a real Young Liberal thank-you for Arnie
. . . cause this country's sure gonna hear from him.
(*Cheers*) O.K. gang. I just want to give you a rundown
now on the agenda of tonight's meeting. I think most of us
will be heading into public service, probably at the federal
level, so I'd like to set aside an hour or so where we could

all kick around a few ideas on different government areas where, with a little know-how, it's possible to pick up some extra bread. Things like public works where you might be able to put a contract into the right hands and earn yourself a kickback here and there. And Indian Affairs looks pretty good, too. It seems to me an enterprising young guy should be able to divert a real nice bundle in that field without our redskin brothers even knowing what hit em.

Now, gang, at nine o'clock we'll have our usual social break. There'll be a bar set up at the rear of the Hall. Beer fifty cents and liquor a buck. But, believe me, if you guys can't figure out a way of sneaking a free drink when the bartender's got his back turned then you better switch right now to some sucker career like teaching or social work. (*Loud cheers and laughter*)

THE GIRL THAT I MARRY

Armed with the gift of hindsight, we can all look back now and marvel at those Far Eastern astrologers, soothsayers and fortune tellers who, months ago, all predicted that Pierre Trudeau would be married within a year. When one chap in Ceylon even went so far as to describe the future bride as "cultured, gifted and exceedingly beautiful" we all wondered who she could possibly be.

THE SCENE:

The foyer of the National Arts Centre in Ottawa, crowded with the arrival of a first night audience.

COLLISTER: This is Ron Collister reporting from Ottawa. Here, in the foyer of the National Arts Centre we have just watched the official government limousine pull up to the doors and deliver the Prime Minister who is attending tonight's performance. Among the three hundred or more first-nighters jammed into the foyer this evening, there's more than usual degree of excitement and anticipation which normally greets the arrival of Mr. Trudeau. The thought uppermost in the minds of all of us here and, indeed, in the minds of Canadians everywhere is: "What are we to make of these persistent prognostications that the Prime Minister will be married within the year?" Well, in just a moment, I hope to be able to learn from Mr. Trudeau just what his reaction to all this is. He's just moving over this way now. Excuse me, sir. . . .

TRUDEAU: Oh, hello there.

COLLISTER: Would you care to tell us, sir, how you feel about these predictions widely held among Far Eastern astrologers, that you'll be married within the year?

TRUDEAU: Well, I suppose it makes good copy . . . uh . . . sells newspapers . . . and if your I.Q. happens to be under 65 you could put some faith in them.

COLLISTER: One astrologer in Ceylon has even gone so far as to describe the lady you'll marry. He says she'll be "cultured, gifted and exceedingly beautiful." And, of course, sir, a lot of people are taking this to mean Miss Barbra Streisand.

TRUDEAU: Well, apart from all other considerations, I think if I were to marry Miss Streisand I would be leaving myself open to the criticism that I married her just because she's famous.

COLLISTER: Then there really is no possibility of your marrying this year?

TRUDEAU: Well, I wouldn't say that exactly. There is a lady whom I've seen off and on . . . I haven't taken her out publicly, of course . . . but she is perhaps the only lady I've met who possesses the five basic qualities which I consider essential in a woman and which I've always looked for in vain.

COLLISTER: I don't suppose, sir, you'd be willing to divulge her name?

TRUDEAU: Certainly not. I think that would be quite unchivalrous and grossly embarrassing for the lady in question.

COLLISTER: Well, would you be willing, sir, to divulge these five qualities you referred to?

TRUDEAU: Yes, I think I could do that much without giving anything away. Unlike a lot of men, I've never put any great stress on beauty, wealth, fame and all the other shallow, materialistic considerations. I suppose you could call me oldfashioned because of the simple, inward quality of female attractiveness which has always appealed to me. This lady, for example, fascinates me simply because she's . . . well, she's . . . uh. . . .

COLLISTER: No need to rush, sir. We can always clear the National News.

TRUDEAU: Well, if you'll just give me a moment, Ron, I'm sure these five qualities will come to me. She's . . . uh . . . she's . . . uh. . . . (*He begins to hum a familiar melody.*) Yes, that's it . . . she's gracious! (*more humming*) And . . . uh . . . and . . . noble! (*humming continues*) Ah, yes, now they're coming to me . . . The last three qualities are victorious . . . happy . . . and . . . uh . . . glorious. Mind you, I'm not saying I'll marry her within the year . . . these things take time. Well, I think that's as far as I want to go, Ron. I'm sorry I had to be secretive about all this . . . I wish I could have divulged her name but I think you'll appreciate there are still some of the old-fashioned virtues of . . . well, modesty, integrity . . . that I feel we should try to cling to in a world that seems to put so much stress on materialism and self-aggrandizement.

THE MUNRO DOCTORIN'

It's always refreshing to see a politician openly admit a mistake. Some months ago an unusual directive was sent to the Indians of Brandon, Manitoba, from the federal Health Department. It informed the Indians that, henceforth, unless their children had a better than average education which would lead to a vocation where good teeth would be an asset, no free dental care would be given. Questioned in the House about it, Health Minister John Munro candidly admitted the directive was "a mistake."

THE SCENE:
The office of the Health Minister in Ottawa.

COLLISTER: This is Ron Collister reporting from the office of the federal minister of Health and Welfare, Mr. John Munro. Sir, I'm sure a lot of Canadians were quite appalled to learn of this strange directive from your department to the Indians of Brandon, Manitoba . . . a document which, in effect, denied the basic right of dental care to all but a small handful of Indian children.

MUNRO: Ron, there was nobody more appalled by that directive than I was.

COLLISTER: Well, I noticed that when questioned about it on the floor of the House you did call it a mistake.

MUNRO: A stupid, idiotic, unforgivable mistake, Ron, that's caused me and my entire department a heck of a lot of embarrassment.

COLLISTER: How could a thing like this have happened, sir?

MUNRO: Well, let me try to explain, Ron. Oh! Would you happen to have a cigaret on you, Ron?

COLLISTER: I'm sorry, sir, I don't smoke.

MUNRO: Oh, no! ! !

COLLISTER: I think I might be able to help you though.

MUNRO (*desperately*): You do?

COLLISTER: Yes. I just noticed there are three full ones still going in your ash tray and you still have two in your mouth.

MUNRO: Oh, for heaven's sake! I guess this whole business has just got me so darn upset. Well, anyway Ron, let me begin by saying that I hope Canadians are fair-minded enough to recognize that this is a pretty big department. It takes hundreds of cigarets . . . er . . . people to run it. There are departments within departments . . . a complicated chain of command . . . overlapping spheres of authority . . . in short, a lot of the disadvantages of the bureaucratic system. Now, all I can say, Ron, is that somewhere along the line . . . and I apologize for this . . . a perfectly fair and reasonable directive, that didn't even have anything to do with *dental* health, got all twisted and distorted and came out as this piece of discriminatory idiocy that's caused all this deserved criticism. I've spent three sleepless days and nights tracking this thing down and believe me, Ron, heads are going to roll. I also want to thank you, Ron, and the CBC for giving me the opportunity to explain and apologize to the Canadian public.

COLLISTER: Well, I think you've managed to show us, Mr. Munro, that your department isn't quite as inhumane and callous as this unintentional and unfortunate mistake might have led us to believe.

MUNRO: Thank you, Ron.

COLLISTER: One final question, sir. What *was* the original directive?

MUNRO: Well, as I said, Ron, it wasn't even connected with *dental* health. It was just an honest attempt to streamline and speed up the treatment of physical injuries among Indian children. We felt, for example, that a lot of time and energy could be saved if the doctor only treated hand injuries in cases where the Indian child was obviously going to be a concert pianist and foot injuries only where the child would be one day joining Canada's Olympic track team or the Royal Winnipeg Ballet.

COLLISTER: Well, thank you, Mr. Munro, for setting the record straight. . . .

MUNRO: Thank you, Ron.

COLLISTER: . . . and clearing up a misunderstanding.

MUNRO: I appreciate the chance, Ron.

COLLISTER: It certainly shows that . . .

MUNRO: Indeed it does, Ron.

COLLISTER: . . . the best laid plans of mice and men. . . .

MUNRO: That's a great line, Ron.

COLLISTER: . . . gang aft agley.

MUNRO: I wish I'd thought of that, Ron. Believe me, you sure know how to use your mouth . . . If you ever need any free dental care, Ron. . . .

HOW YA GONNA KEEP EM UP ON THE HILL AFTER THEY'VE SEEN THE WEST?

Farm communities in Saskatchewan that have lived through drought, erosion and grasshoppers probably still haven't recovered from the shock of last February when, during the two days that shook the West, Pierre Trudeau and his cabinet ministers moseyed in to bring federal government closer to the people. Places that hadn't seen a federal politician in years were knee-deep in smiling, hand-shaking cabinet ministers.

THE SCENE:

On the farm of Orville Goomer in Moose Groin, Saskatchewan.

TRUDEAU: Well, Mr. Goomer, my cabinet ministers and I will be moving along shortly to visit some of the other farmers in the area and try to help them with their problems but, before we go, I just wanted to say how much we've appreciated our fifteen-minute visit with you.

ORVILLE: Well, sir, she was a bit of a shock, I don't mind tellin' ya, when I seen all you fellas rollin in here in them big, fancy cars. Now, about them seventeen White Leghorns you fellas run over comin' up the front drive. . . .

TRUDEAU: I don't suppose you see too many federal politicians passing this way, Mr. Goomer.

ORVILLE: Nope. As a matter of fact I thought you was Mackenzie King.

TRUDEAU: My goodness . . . he hasn't been around for quite a few years.

ORVILLE: Yep, one of your boys was tellin' me that. Well, lookit, about them White Leghorns, Mr. St. Laurent. . . .

TRUDEAU: Uh . . . Trudeau . . . Pierre Trudeau.

ORVILLE: Oh. Well, lookit Pierre, I got these here seventeen flattened out Leghorns on the drive, and another thing I wanted to mention before ya cleared out, you know when ya jumped up on my big Massey-Ferguson there a few minutes ago and insisted on drivin' her.

TRUDEAU: Oh yes.

ORVILLE: Well I figure it's gonna cost me about $300 to fix up that hole where ya wheeled her into the side of the barn and about another $300 where ya come out on the far side.

TRUDEAU: Yes, we've all had so much fun, Mr. Goomer, doing things we'd never have a chance to do in Ottawa. Well, just look at my External Affairs minister, Mitchell Sharp, over there . . . he's never had a chance to milk a cow before.

ORVILLE: Well, I was gonna mention that. Would ya ask him not to try shovin' that pail under that critter's belly . . . (*Angry whinny*) cause that's a Clydesdale and like as not he'll put a hoof right into that fella's eardrum. Now, I also wanted to mention the implement shed. . . .

TRUDEAU: Uh . . . the implement shed?

ORVILLE: Yep. One of your boys went pokin' around in there. Don't know whether it was the fella with all the sparks blowin' outta his pipe. . . .

TRUDEAU: Uh . . . that would be Mr. Benson.

ORVILLE: . . . or it might of been the one with the tanned fingers and the three cigarets goin' all at once.

TRUDEAU: Uh . . . that would be Health Minister Munro.

ORVILLE: Well, whoever it was, about two minutes after he come out the whole place went up in flames and I'm out about $12,000.

TRUDEAU: Oh dear . . . something's got to be done about that! Just hold on a moment, Mr. Goomer. (*shouting*) Gentlemen! Would you all come over here, please!

[*The ministers crowd in chattering among themselves.*]

TRUDEAU: Look, I've just learned that Mr. Goomer has sustained a considerable financial loss as a result of the hospitality he's extended to all of us. Now I think the least we can do is make a group effort . . . all pitch in together so to speak and show him that we're standing behind him one hundred per cent.

ORVILLE: Well now, that's sure mighty decent. Actually there's no rush. I mean if ya wanna wait and mail a cheque from Ottawa. I sure don't wanna leave you short.

TRUDEAU: All together now gentlemen and let's see what we can come up with.

CHORUS OF
MINISTERS: More of us do more for you in the Commons
House of Commons . . . House of Commons.
More of us do more . . .

WILL YOU PLEASE GET OFF THE
FRANCOPHONE?

*Like a child discovering a new toy, the federal gov-
ernment this past year has gleefully clasped to its
breast a new word . . . "Francophone." Almost overnight, the old expression "French-speaking Canadian" has vanished and if you're really with it, like Mr.
Sharp and Mr. Drury, you now use the term "Francophone Canadian."*

THE SCENE:

A CBC National News item. From Ottawa, using
English sub-titles, Norman DePoe is talking to
Mitchell Sharp.

DEPOE: Mr. Sharp, it's generally conceded that you were one
of the first to introduce Canadians to this new word . . .
Francophone."

SHARP: Well, my goodness, Norman, it's not really a new
word. You see, as acting Prime Minister from time to time,
I've had quite a bit of spare time on my hands and I en-
countered this word while I was doing a crossword puzzle
in the House one day. I rather liked the sound of it. It has
quite a ring to it.

DEPOE: Well, Mr. Sharp. . . .

SHARP: Uh, could you hold it just a second, Norman? That was
a little pun there. Francophone . . . it has quite a *ring* to it?

DEPOE: Oh, I'm sorry.

SHARP: That's all right, Norman. I just wanted to give the folks
a chance to get it. Carry on.

DEPOE: Well, I was just wondering, sir, can Canadians look
forward to any more new words coming into vogue in
government circles?

SHARP: Oh, my goodness, Norman, I should say so. This is just
the beginning. We're just starting to become aware of the
importance of linguistics in politics. You see, starting with

"Francophone," which means "French speaking", and using it as our root, we're going to be able to categorize just about every single person who speaks French.

DEPOE: Just how do you mean, sir?

SHARP: Well, let's take an example. A French-speaking Canadian who also speaks Spanish would be a *Franco* Francophone.

DEPOE: I see.

SHARP: A French-speaking Canadian who behaves strangely . . . sort of a ding-a-ling . . . would be a Princess Phone.

DEPOE: Well, that's very interesting, Mr. Sharp. Thank you for. . . .

SHARP: A French-speaking Canadian who also likes ballet would be a Celia Francophone.

DEPOE: Yes, well I'm afraid that's all the. . . .

SHARP: A French-speaking Canadian lady who has grandchildren would, of course, be a grama-phone.

DEPOE Again, sir, thank you for. . . .

SHARP: A young French-speaking female with a husky, sultry voice would be a sexophone. There are just endless possibilities, Norman, there's a whole new exciting field opening up here which I hope will be a real challenge to some of the brighter minds in Ottawa.

READY OR NOT YOU MUST BE CAUGHT — NO FAIR HANGING AROUND THE COAST

Minister Jack Davis certainly seems to be running a "no-nonsense" Federal Fisheries Department. Fair warning has been given to the world that any foreign fishing vessel caught operating in Canadian waters will be subject to "hot" or "armed" pursuit, if it should attempt to run from fishery patrol vessels.

Through wisps of a slowly lifting fog, a Canadian fishery patrol vessel, its engines labouring, slowly limps into port.

FIRST OFFICER: We're coming alongside, Captain!

CAPTAIN: Right, number one. (*shouts*) Hard astern . . . stand by to secure fore and aft!

VOICE (*off*): Hard astern . . . stand by to secure fore and aft!

[*Bells and assorted sounds from the wheelhouse.*]

CAPTAIN: Well, number one, that's what you call a wild-goose chase. Boy, I wish we could have got our hands on that Russian trawler!

FIRST OFFICER: Well, captain, we almost got em. If we only could have coaxed a few more knots out of this patrol vessel.

CAPTAIN: I suppose I should have given up when we got outside that twelve-mile limit. How long were we out there, do you figure?

FIRST OFFICER: Gosh, it must be over a week, sir.

CAPTAIN: Boy, if I could have closed range on that trawler I'd have opened up with every gun we've got . . . show em what we mean by hot pursuit. Hey, what part of the coast do you figure this is?

FIRST OFFICER: Gee, we've logged so many miles chasing that Russian trawler, captain, zigzagging, back-tracking, circling, and with our navigational gear on the fritz I'd have to go by dead reckoning and say it's Port Alberni.

CAPTAIN: Yeah, I think you're right. Certainly looks like Port Alberni.

FIRST OFFICER: Let's ask that guy up there on the jetty.

CAPTAIN: O.K. . . . Ahoy, up there! We've been at sea for over a week giving hot pursuit to some stupid Russian trawler. We've lost our bearings. Could you tell me if this is Port Alberni?

RUSSIAN (*off*): Port Alberni? Do not know Port Alberni. Dees place . . . Murmansk . . . home base . . . Red Baltic fleet.

FIRST OFFICER: Murmansk!

CAPTAIN: Good lord!

RUSSIAN: What means dees . . . hot porsuit you geev Russian trawler?

CAPTAIN (*swallowing hard*): No, no. You apparently misunderstood me, sir. I said "hot *pea* soup." You see, we're with the seagoing arm of the Salvation Army in Canada. (*low and urgent*) Let's get this tub out of here, fast! (*up full*) We're just come through a pretty hard winter . . . lotta flu going around. (*low*) Tell the engine-room to get this thing moving. (*up full*) So we've been sort of just cruising around handing out hot pea soup to all our brothers in navy blue from other lands . . . (*low*) Get the crew to sing hymns . . . (*up full*) in the belief that we are, indeed, our brother's keeper . . . (*low*) Oh, my gawd . . . throw your coat over those guns will you? . . . what's keeping that damn engine-room? . . .

THE STRANGE CASE OF THE VANISHING MILLIONS

Domestic postage in Canada, which jumped to seven cents not long ago, may even go to eight cents the government warns. The increase, we are told, is needed to offset a deficit of 110 million dollars which has been forecast for this year. The prolonged mail strike of 1970 accounted for thirty million of that deficit but no one has explained yet what caused the other eighty million.

THE SCENE:

The stirring strains of "O Canada" slowly fade, and onto the screen of every TV set in the country appears the smiling, confident face of our Prime Minister.

PRIME MINISTER: I wish to thank the Canadian Broadcasting Corporation for enabling me to speak to all Canadians on this occasion and to explain to them, in all honesty and candour, why the post office is facing a deficit of 110 million dollars this year. This, of course, would normally be the duty of the minister responsible, Mr. Jean Pierre Coté. Mr. Coté, however, feels that the explanation is so bizarre that Canadians might not believe him. I, on the contrary, have always had great faith in the humanity, compassion and understanding of Canadians and their sincere belief that "to err is human, to forgive divine."

We in Canada produce more new postage stamps than any other country . . . I believe the average is one every two days. About a year ago, we came to the conclusion that if we could honour moose, beaver, Canada geese and so forth, then we should certainly be able to honour a Canadian who has become a legend in his time. And so, with his seventy-fifth birthday coming up, plans were laid to salute and commemorate John Diefenbaker on our six-cent stamp. Since the most costly part of bringing out a new stamp is the engraving, it was felt that a great saving would accrue to the taxpayers of this country if we were to take one of the many engravings we already had of Her Majesty and, employing the skills of the best engravers in Canada, simply convert her likeness into that of John Diefenbaker. This task was carried out with consumate skill and artistry. Six million stamps were run off and sent to post offices all across Canada for release and sale on Mr. Diefenbaker's seventy-fifth birthday. However, on the very eve of the release date, it was discovered that, due to a tiny oversight on the part of the engraver, there appeared just below Mr. Diefenbaker's sternly thrust jaw a pearl necklace and the definite outlines of a female bust. Frantic long-distance calls to every post office in Canada fortunately resulted in every stamp being re-called . . . with the exception of one single stamp which, by the cruelest quirk of fate, had already been purchased by Mr. Diefenbaker. He forthwith launched proceedings against the post office, asking forty million dollars in damages for defamation of character . . . an amount which we feel certain he will win. By an even stranger quirk of fate, he used the stamp on a letter which he sent off to Her Majesty complaining about the way we were handling the unemployment situation. She, therefore, after seeing her upper torso and necklace surmounted by the head of Mr. Diefenbaker, is likewise suing for an identical amount of forty million. This, then, makes a grand total of eighty million and, of course, the other thirty million of the deficit is due, as we all know, to last summer's postal strike. I ask you all to remain calm, trusting in God and the Liberal party.

GIVE US A NAME AND WE'LL FINISH THE JOB

A new, government anti-pollution bill now enables Fisheries Minister Jack Davis to levy fines against the industrial barons of this country who, until now, have been polluting our environment with impunity. In sending him into the ring against these captains of industry, thank goodness, the government is at least giving him a new prestigious and authoritative title . . . Minister of Environment!

THE SCENE:

The office of the Prime Minister.

TRUDEAU (*at sound of knocking*): Yes, come in. (*door opens*)

DAVIS: You wanted to see me, Mr. Prime Minister?

TRUDEAU: Uh . . . yes . . . uh . . . thank you for dropping by . . . uh . . . pull up a chair. Yes, I've been examining this new letterhead you've had run off for use in your department, Mr. Davis. I presume this is the stationery you'll be using when you notify offending industrialists that you plan to fine them two hundred thousand dollars.

DAVIS: That's correct, Mr. Prime Minister.

TRUDEAU: Well, look, I think your official title up here on the top of each sheet, "Minister of Environment," lends sufficient weight and authority. I don't think there's really any need to include this photograph of yourself dressed in a G-string and holding these thunderbolts in your clenched fist. And these little feathered wings coming out of your ankles . . . it's a bit theatrical.

DAVIS: Now just a second, Mr. Prime Minister. I realize you've bestowed on me one of the most impressive titles a cabinet minister ever had—Minister of Environment—but you've also given me one of the toughest jobs. The men that I'm going to have to fine and intimidate are the big tycoons, the commercial barons of this nation. I could conceivably lock horns with magnates like E.P. Taylor, K.C. Irving or some of those tough West Coast lumber moguls . . . men who are used to *giving* orders, not taking them.

TRUDEAU: Yes, but as soon as they see your new title up there on the letterhead, it'll throw them off guard . . . take a lot of the fight out of them.

DAVIS: Yes, but sooner or later my own name is bound to come up . . . Jack Davis. I mean it's pretty plebeian, pretty run-of-the-mill . . . it's not exactly awe-inspiring . . . I can't see it making men's blood run cold. It's certainly not going to intimidate a guy like K.C. Irving.

TRUDEAU: Well, what do you suggest?

DAVIS: Well, if you're not going to let me use that photograph then I've got to legally change my name.

TRUDEAU: Well, I have no objections. What did you have in mind?

DAVIS: I've been giving it some thought and I kind of like . . . Minister of Environment . . . Hari Krishna.

TRUDEAU: No, no. I think we're going to have to try to avoid vulgar pretension; I think you should at least retain your own *first* name.

DAVIS: Well, let's see. There's . . . Jack Manitou, Jack Hitler. . . .

TRUDEAU: No, no. I think we should be striving for something thats' . . . well . . . symbolic. Would you consider . . . Jack Spratt?

DAVIS: Jack Spratt!

TRUDEAU: Yes, after all *he* kept the platter clean just the way you're going to keep our air and water clean.

DAVIS: Gee, it's not bad. Could you pass me over your phone for a second. I just want to try it out . . . give it a dummy run . . . see if it feels comfortable. (*He picks up the phone.*) "Hello? Mr. K.C. Irving? This is the Minister of Environment, Jack Spratt, speaking. Now, about those logs you've got down there plugging up the St. John River, how would you just like to get your fat wallet out and. . . ." No! I don't like it! It doesn't feel comfortable. If I'm going to take on these giants I'm gonna need something a lot better than "Jack Spratt."

TRUDEAU: Wait a minute. You just gave me an idea. How about . . . Jack Beanstalk? Try that one.

DAVIS: "Hello? K.C. Irving? Well, look fella, this is the Minister of Environment . . . Jack Beanstalk . . . speaking, and I'm afraid I'm going to have to cut you down to size. That's right, fella, I'm after your golden goose!" Yeah! Yeah! I like it! I like it!

TRUDEAU: It certainly has a ring to it.

DAVIS: Yep, I'll buy that one!

TRUDEAU: I don't really think you'll do any better.

DAVIS: You're right!

TRUDEAU: It's sort of a forthright, no-nonsense name.

DAVIS: Yeah, it's just great! Jack Beanstalk! The All Canadian Environment Minister! Wow! Wonderful . . . wonderful . . . just great!

BROWSING THROUGH THE NEWS

An agricultural scientist in the U.S. claims that cattle can be brought to market weight in seventy days by feeding them old newspapers. If mixed with soybean and molasses, several newspapers a day can be digested by a cow's stomach.

THE SCENE:

The Ontario Agricultural College in Guelph. In one of the livestock barns Professor Alvin Bunn is being interviewed for CBC radio by roving reporter, Ernest Effort.

ERNEST: Professor Bunn, you've devoted a lifetime to bovine dietary research. Do you think it's nutritionally feasible to feed newspapers to cows?

BUNN: Well, Ernie, we bin lookin' into this for the past three years now and believe me, there's a lot of questions still unanswered.

ERNEST: Such as?

BUNN: Well, when you go messin' around with newsprint in a cow's diet you can't always predict the results. Some do just fine. Others have strange side effects. Now you take that big Hereford lyin' on her side over there not movin'. Last Friday, she polished off twelve copies of Pierre Berton's *National Dream* . . . Been lyin' like that ever since.

ERNEST: Is she dead?

BUNN: No. The vet says she's comitose . . . just lies there dreamin', sort of like Snow White. We may have to get Pierre out here to kiss her . . . see if that'll do anything. Now over there in that stall, that big Holstein . . . she's another strange case. Her name's Big Doreen.

ERNEST (*Walking toward her*): She's a fine looking animal. [*Angry bovine bellow.*]

BUNN: My golly, don't go near her! She'd as lief stick her horns through ya as look at ya. I used to be able to do anything with that cow . . . milk her, vaccinate her, take her temperature . . . and all she'd do was ogle me with them big, limpid, brown eyes. Sometimes she'd even nuzzle me with her big, soft, runny nose.

ERNEST: Well, what on earth happened to her?

BUNN: Doreen ate four copies of that darn book, *The Second Sex*, by Simone de Bovine, and would you believe it she won't let. . . .

ERNEST: Uh, de Beauvoir.

BUNN: What?

ERNEST: Simone de Beauvoir.

BUNN: Well, anyways, she won't let a man within ten feet of her now. We have to get one of our girl students to feed her.

ERNEST: How long does it take you here at O.A.C. to bring a cow to market weight?

BUNN: Depends. Seventy days if they're eating newspapers, course we can cut that down to ten if we put them on *Reader's Digest.*

ERNEST: Well, Professor, I'm afraid my reaction to all this isn't really scientific and I hope you won't think I'm belittling your efforts, but I find it's quite humorous to watch all these cows here munching books and newspapers.

BUNN (*Quite hurt*): Feel like laughin' do ya?

ERNEST: Well, yes.

BUNN: Strange you should mention that. I was eating my lunch in here yesterday . . . had my little dog with me . . . and *he* laughed to see such fun.

ERNEST: For heaven's sake!

BUNN: And I'll tell you another strange thing . . . my fork ran away with the spoon.

ERNEST: Did it really?

BUNN (*Exploding*): Oh, clear outta here will ya. Darn CBC reporters . . . wastin' my time . . . stupid bunch . . . git out . . . git out.

YOU CAN LEAD A HORSE TO WATER BUT...

The Tory advisors whose job it is to improve the television image of leader Robert Stanfield made an important discovery in late November of 1970. Mr. Stanfield, they concluded, looks better standing up than sitting down on TV and so he was advised not to sit down.

THE SCENE:

In the corner of a CBC television studio, two of Mr. Stanfield's advisors wait for the program "Encounter" to go on air. The panel of hard-bitten press pros are seated but Mr. Stanfield, looking like the Maid of Orleans, stands uncomfortably in front of them.

ADVISOR ONE: Frankly, Jim, I don't like this added strain we're putting on Bob. I feel we should let him appear on TV whatever way is most comfortable for him.

ADVISOR TWO: Are you kidding, Ted? Haven't you noticed the difference it makes when he's standing up? When he sits down, he just seems to fold up like a two-dollar suitcase. His voice goes right down inside his jacket.

ADVISOR ONE: I'm not denying that, Jim. I just feel that when Bob's up against guys like Charles Lynch, Ron Collister and Norm DePoe . . . guys that are doing their best to shaft him with real tough questions . . . he shouldn't have to contend with distractions.

ADVISOR TWO: You mean the battery in his right shoe?

ADVISOR ONE: Well, gee, how would you like to get a shock through your foot while you're trying to stick-handle your way through a tough question?

ADVISOR TWO: Look, Ted . . . it's only 100 volts, more or less, and I never juice him unless he forgets and starts sliding into a chair.

ADVISOR ONE: Well, you were at him a coupla minutes ago about using his hands.

ADVISOR TWO: Ted, you just can't leave the hands hangin' there! You know how effective hands can be. Some guys can say more with their hands than they can with their mouth. Well, I mean . . . look at Trudeau! Geez, he's like a windmill. Now you take Bob. Last time he made effective use of his hands in public was when he peeled that banana at the leadership convention.

ADVISOR ONE: But it's just another thing for him to have to remember. I think we're giving him too much of a load. He could crack up, you know!

ADVISOR TWO: Aw, come on Ted! As far as the hands go, Bob doesn't have to do a thing! You see, I've got this fine thread around both wrists. The two threads run up into the lighting grid up there and one of the stage hands says he'll work the hands for ten bucks. They'll be flyin' all over the place and Bob won't have to worry about 'em.

ADVISOR ONE: Well, I still say it's disconcerting. It's too much all at once. Look at him over there in front of that panel of vultures! His eyes are glazed . . . he looks catatonic!
[The director's voice booms into the studio from the control room.]

DIRECTOR: All right, everybody . . . quiet on the set . . . we're going in five . . . stand by . . . cue announcer!

ANNOUNCER: The CBC presents . . . Encounter! To-night, our guest is Mr. Robert Stanfield, leader of the opposition. Ron Collister begins the questioning.

COLLISTER: Mr. Stanfield, you've had a lot to say about the way the Liberals are combatting unemployment in this country. Just how would *you* go about it?

STANFIELD: Uh . . . well . . . that's . . . uh . . . that's a good question, Ron . . . uh . . . let me just say this. . . .
[As he starts to slump he gets the juice while the stagehand yanks the threads. With arms flailing and body twitching he continues.]

STANFIELD: Uh . . . let me . . . uh . . . let me put it this way . . . uh . . . When you wish upon a star. . . .

ADVISOR ONE: Jim! My God ... it's happening.

STANFIELD: Uh ... makes ... uh ... makes no difference who you are ... uh ...

ADVISOR ONE: Jim! He's cracking!

ADVISOR TWO (*Hissing across the set*): Bob! Bob! Snap out of it!

STANFIELD: ... Uh ... everything your heart desires, Ron ... uh ... will come your way....

ADVISOR ONE: We're in big trouble, Jim!

ADVISOR TWO: Don't tell me! Hey you up there! Let go of those goddam threads!

ADVISOR ONE: Watch it, Jim! That went out over the air!

STANFIELD: ... Like a bolt from out the blue ... uh ... fate stepped in and ... uh ...

ANNOUNCER: This is the CBC television network.

A MAN'S AMBITION SHOULD EXCEED HIS GRASP

Dissolution of the Commonwealth seemed a strong possibility when the member countries sent their prime ministers to the Singapore Conference in January, 1971, to discuss the sale of British arms to South Africa. Before leaving Ottawa, Prime Minister Trudeau made a plea to all Canadians not to expect him to perform miracles.

THE SCENE:

Inside the government *Jet Star* as it takes off from Ottawa bearing the Prime Minister on his tour of Asia and the Singapore Conference.

AIDE: Well, Mr. Prime Minister . . . we're off! I certainly hope, when we come back from this one, the Commonwealth will still be entact!

TRUDEAU: Yes, indeed. There could be a lot of fireworks over Britain's insistence on selling arms to South Africa.

AIDE: We'll just have to wait and see . . . could be a very sticky wicket. Oh . . . uh . . . sir? If there's nothing pressing at the moment, I thought I might just slip to the back of the aircraft and catch forty winks. Would that be all right?

TRUDEAU: Hmmmmm. I was going to ask you to run over this speech with me. It's fairly brief but I would like to get a timing on it.

AIDE: Oh, certainly sir!

TRUDEAU: Are you ready?

AIDE: Fire away, sir.

TRUDEAU (*Reading*): In my considered opinion, it would be a wonderful achievement if you could forget such things as union, cohesion and togetherness. I would strongly recommend . . . nay, even command . . . that you split up, divide and go your separate ways. I would earnestly welcome a rift that would separate you into two distinct segments.

AIDE: Excuse me, sir . . . forgive me for saying this . . . but isn't that a rather strange and ill-advised speech to be delivering to the Commonwealth prime ministers at a crucial time such as this?

TRUDEAU: Oh, this isn't the speech I'm delivering to them!

AIDE: It isn't?

TRUDEAU: No, the Commonwealth speech is in my brief case. I just thought I'd like to have this one handy when I get to the shores of the Red Sea. I thought, perhaps, I'd try it out on the waves.

AIDE: Sir . . . you just finished making a plea to all Canadians not to expect you to perform any. . . .

TRUDEAU: Well, I don't think there's anything to lose! Probably nothing will even come of it but if I should be able to bring it off, it certainly won't do me any harm in the next election. I think it's only human nature to want to improve one's image.

AIDE: Really, sir! I think you should concentrate on the Commonwealth Conference! And while I'm at it . . . I'd like to point out that the loaf of bread you stuck in your suitcase is going to leave crumbs all through your underwear and by the time those five fish get to India, I'd hate to think what your shirts are going to smell like! Now if you'll take my advice, why don't you just relax on this trip, do the best you can and don't be so competitive!

IT CAN'T HAPPEN HERE

Early this year, the U.S. army chemically sprayed and killed a flock of three million blackbirds which had taken up residence in a pine forest near an army installation in Tennessee. Can you imagine the hue and cry if this had happened in our country?

[*Sound of gulls. Bow wash. The throbbing engines of a ship.*]

OLD SALT: Well, now, when you stick that microphone under me nose, boy, and ask me to sound off about all them millions of birds and what was done to em by the U.S. army . . . I'll have to warn yez that I'm more than a little prejudiced. Ya see, I've always loved birds. Always had 'em as pets . . . budgies, canaries or some such thing. Had an old parrot once too . . . he was with me for over twenty years and a better friend than most humans would be. And the gulls . . . God, I've lived with those wild, haunting cries in me ears for most of me life. And the hours of pleasure they've given me on the long watches . . .

soarin' and wheelin' . . . and a hell of a lot freer than most of us can ever be. And ya know, I've never seen much point to judgin' birds by human standards . . . what I mean is, I don't give a damn if a bird's got pretty plumage or makes beautiful songs. To me, a bird is a bird. I don't care if it's a nightingale or a blackbird. But I think what we have in this business of the U.S. army makin' wholesale slaughter of them blackbirds, I think it's just another sign of what's happenin' to folks down there. I mean ya can't expect a people who've done what they've done in Vietnam with their napalm, their flamethrowers and their chemical defoliants . . . you can't expect 'em to get too worked up over the murder of three million blackbirds.

VOICE ALOFT: Captain! Off the starboard bow!

OLD SALT: Oh, you'll have to stand clear of me way, boy. The look-out's spotted somethin'. Ah, that's them all right! The main herd! All right, lads . . . over the side and club anything that's movin' . . . skin em as fast as ya can . . . there's 50,000 pelts out there if ya shake a leg. Hurry lads . . . don't let em get away . . . over the side every man Jack of ya.

REPORTER: This is Leslie Lovelace of the CBC returning you to our studios from the ice floes of the St. Lawrence Gulf.

THE LONG WINTER

The frontiers of men's minds were rolled back appreciably last winter by the Toronto Humane Society. At the time, the Society, which normally finds homes for about fifty kittens every weekend, was experiencing an unusual shortage of kittens. Officials deduced that severe cold spells cause a decline in cat pregnancies.

THE SCENE:

A middle aged lady rocks to and fro in front of a cosy fire listening to the chilling sound of a howling blizzard. Her cat sleeps by the hearth and, across the room, her husband wears an overcoat as he peruses the evening paper.

LADY (*Singing*): Good King Wenceslas looked out
         On the feast of Stephen,
         When the snow lay . . .
(*A loud plaintive meow from the cat.*) Mercy, what's the matter Fluffy? Did pussy have a bad dream? There now, puss, you just put your little head down and go back to sleep. (*Another meow.*) What's the matter with mother's little girl? Surely you don't want to go outside, Fluffy. It's such a terrible night out there. Look at the snow all over the windows and just listen to that wind, puss. Oh, it's terrible out there tonight, puss. Only bad cats are out there to-night . . . caterwauling and getting into goodness knows what kind of trouble. Good kittens, like our Fluffy, they'll all be sleeping at home in front of the fire with mummy and daddy.

MAN: Oh, Daisy, that's sick!

LADY: Now look, dear, I don't want to go all through this again!

MAN: But wouldn't it be simpler . . . wouldn't it be better for all of us . . . if you just took that cat to the vet. I mean if you don't want her goin' out and gettin' pregnant, then for Pete's sake get her spayed.

LADY: Oh, yes! The typical chauvinistic male . . . put the onus on the female every time! No, thank you just the same . . . we'll do it my way. I feel if people aren't willing to put themselves out a tiny bit, to make a little effort to safeguard the well-being of their pets, then they shouldn't be allowed to have pets!

MAN: But Daisy, I've just about had my fill of sittin' here every blessed night in this darn overcoat, with a fire on, listenin' to you croonin' carols to that cat.

LADY: Stop whining and get the aerosol can. Those windows need some more snow on them . . . and while you're on your feet, you might as well give the gramaphone a few cranks . . . that wind record is startin' to run down.

MAN: Oh, all right, but mark my words, Daisy! When that cat finds out that it's midsummer out there it's gonna be pretty darn resentful.

LADY: Oh, shut up! (*Cat meows.*) Not you, sweetheart! You just go bye-bye now . . . that's a good kitty.
Good King Wenceslas looked out
On the feast of Stephen
When the snow. . . .

THE SPECIALIST

Alberta seemed to kick off a chain reaction of eyebrow raising among provincial Ministers of Health, when a report was tabled in the legislature revealing that, while the average annual income of doctors was $46,430 ten doctors in that province managed to earn $200,000.

THE SCENE:

The operating room of an Alberta hospital. The chief OR nurse is staring in fascination at the nimble hands of the surgeon.

SURGEON: Suture!

CHIEF NURSE: Suture!

SURGEON: Clamp!

CHIEF NURSE: Clamp! ... You know, sir, I just wish every person in Canada could watch those hands of yours. I just can't take my eyes off them.

SURGEON: Thanks, nurse. Yes, I guess some of those whining, griping laymen have no idea of the years of hard work it takes to develop a pair of hands like mine.

CHIEF NURSE: Well, it wasn't *that* so much, doctor, I just . . . well . . . I just. . . .

SURGEON: What are you trying to say, nurse?

CHIEF NURSE: Well, doctor, that gorgeous self-winding watch and gold expansion bracelet . . . and those four sapphire rings . . . they must have cost a fortune!

SURGEON: As a matter of fact they did, nurse, but just you remember . . . I earned every cent of it!

CHIEF NURSE: Oh, certainly doctor!

SURGEON: I don't want to hear any sour grapes!

CHIEF NURSE: Oh, certainly not, doctor!

SURGEON: I've had a belly full of that, believe me, from these laymen. Newspapers, politicians, the general public . . . they all make me sick. They just don't understand how long it's taken me to train these hands to this degree of sureness, swiftness, adroitness and sensitivity and furthermore. . . .

CHIEF NURSE: Excuse me, doctor, I think one of your rings is caught on the muscle fibre there. . . .

SURGEON: Oh . . . thanks . . . geez, I hope I didn't loosen that setting. . . . And furthermore, nurse, if these hands can earn me $200,000 a year, it's none of their damn business. Oh! Hold on, gang. Here we are . . . let me just ease this out . . . boy! no wonder this poor devil had back pains . . . look at the size of that kidney stone!

CHIEF NURSE: Goodness!

ASSISTANT: Nicely done, doctor! Would you like me to close for you?

SURGEON: Are you kidding? This part of the operation's only

worth peanuts! I can only stick this guy for a lousy coupla hundred bucks. Don't you dare close him up. (*Brightly to all present*) All right, gang, who wants to get in on this?

SEVERAL VOICES: Me! Yeah, me too! ! . . . Count me in . . . Me too! . . . Yeah, I'm game!

SURGEON: O.K! O.K! Now, you all know the house rules. Ten bucks a shot. . . . I'll give five to one odds . . . no cheques or IOUs. O.K. Here we go. Now keep your eyes on that kidney stone. I place it under this kidney here . . . move the two kidneys and the gall bladder around a little bit . . . there! O.K. let's start with the scrub nurse.

SCRUB NURSE: Um . . . let me see . . . I think it's under that one, doctor.

SURGEON: Ha, ha! You weren't watching, were you? Too bad about that, nurse. How about you, doctor?

ASSISTANT: Well, gee, it's got to be under the gall bladder!

SURGEON: Voila! Wrong again! Let's see now, that's twenty bucks. Hey, how long is this anaesthetic good for?

ANAESTHESIOLOGIST: I'd say you've got a good ninety minutes before he comes out of it, doctor.

SURGEON: Oh, great! Hey, nurse!

NURSE: Yes, doctor?

SURGEON: Go up into the ampitheatre . . . must be about three hundred young medical students up there . . . tell em I'm offering a special deal . . . only *five* bucks a shot and I'll make it easy for em by only using the kidneys.

NURSE: Not the gall bladder?

SURGEON: No gall bladder! But tell em to hurry and line up in single file at this end of the operating table . . . we've only got about an hour and a half. And remember . . . no cheques . . . no IOUs . . . make sure they know that!

PARTICIPATORY DEMOCRACY

Early in 1971, following charges by two federal MP's that Prime Minister Trudeau had mouthed a four-letter word at them across the floor of the House, there was an indignant outcry from almost every quarter. Trudeau's claim that the word was merely "fuddle-duddle" still didn't satisfy everyone.

THE SCENE:

A turbulent afternoon in the House of Commons. The desk thumping and cries of "Shame, shame!" finally subside to allow the Speaker to be heard.

SPEAKER: In view of the gravity of the situation and the serious nature of the charges which have been levelled at the Right Honourable gentleman, the chair requests the permission of all the Honourable Members to circumvent the normal rules of protocol in order to recognize the lady who now has the floor.

COCKNEY VOICE: Thank you, your eminence, for allowing me to speak on behalf of the entire cleaning staff of Parliament Hill. I think all the honourable chaps present 'ere today know us well enough to realize that we are not what you might call whiners or complainers. We all do our best to keep this place clean and tidy. Whilst you chaps are in your trundle beds or wherever you end up when you leave here . . . I mean that's your business . . . me and the other ladies are quite willing to go about pickin' up cigaret butts, scrapin' stale wads of gum off the seats, sweepin' up chocolate-bar wrappers, popsicle sticks, pop-corn and what have you. 'Owever, I must say that the way things is goin' around 'ere I can foresee our jobs becomin' a bleedin' and intolerable nightmare.

SPEAKER: In just what way, madam?

COCKNEY: Well look, ducks, we don't mind takin' soap and a brush and rubbin' straightforward graphiti off the washroom walls. Good straightforward four-letter words don't bother us none . . . goodness knows we've scrubbed enough of them off in our day . . . but if that bloke over there . . . yes, you! . . . if 'e thinks he can go about writin' things like "fuddle-duddle" on the washroom walls then you can just get yourselves a new cleanin' staff! I mean that's twelve letters compared to four! It's simple arithmetic. If it takes us five minutes to scrub off a regular four-letter word, it'll take fifteen minutes to remove something like "fuddle-duddle"!

SPEAKER: Is the lady implying that the Prime Minister has been writing this on the walls of the men's washroom?

COCKNEY: Not yet, 'e 'asn't. But mark my words . . . 'e will! You show me a foul mouth and I'll show you a graphiti artist every bleedin' time! I want 'im banned from every washroom on Parliament Hill. An ounce of prevention is worth a pound of cure! I mean, there's no point lockin' the barn door after the water's gone under the bridge, is there? If the likes of 'im was to go about writin' "fuddle-duddle" all over the walls, all of us would be workin' twenty-four hours a day. If 'e wants to write four-letter words that's all right with me . . . but I will not put up with none of these twelve-letter obscenities like "fuddle-duddle" or "fiddle-dee-dee" or God knows what other shockin' things 'e 'as tucked away in that Rabelaisian mind of 'is. I want that bloke banned from all the washrooms or you can take your Parliament Hill and staff it . . . with new cleanin' ladies!

[*Desk thumping and cries of "Here, Here!" from opposition benches.*]

The British Army recently established a "tea and sympathy" squad. Made up of colonels, majors and captains, the squad's duty is to comfort lonely army wives whose husbands are away on duty. Though not strictly marriage counsellors, the officers will be expected to discuss the wives' problems over a cup of tea.

THE SCENE:

The private quarters of a young English colonel at Camp Aldershot.

[Sound of tea being poured.]

COLONEL: I'm terribly sorry . . . is it one lump or two you take in your tea?

WIFE: Oh, no thank you, love. I've 'ad three cups already. I'd best be toddlin' 'ome, but it was lovely 'avin' the chance to talk over me problems with you.

COLONEL: Well, that's jolly well what we're here for.

WIFE: 'Ere, do you mind me askin' 'ow you got to be a colonel . . . I mean bein' so young an all, love.

COLONEL: Well, I've had a spot of luck here and and there, you know. Only been in the army three years . . . joined right after Cambridge.

WIFE: Eee . . . not like me poor old 'usband.

COLONEL: You know I must say I find your story quite incredible . . . I mean the fact that your husband could have served the British Army all these years with absolutely no promotion . . . not even to lance corporal. Damn poor show, I must say, especially in view of the high regard in which you say he was held by his commanding officer.

WIFE: Oh, my yes! Why, 'is commandin' officer admitted publicly that 'e wasn't arf the man me 'usband was! I mean that there's official . . . I 'ave that in writin'.

COLONEL: By jove, that strikes me as most unfair.

WIFE: Well, of course, me 'usband wasn't born in this country, you know.

COLONEL: That shouldn't make the slightest bit of difference. And these degrading duties you spoke of . . . running about at the beck and call of everyone in the regiment. That's simply appalling.

WIFE: And 'e never sends me no money 'ome . . . says the army don't pay 'im enough for to keep 'imself.

COLONEL: Well, I shall certainly look into this. Now I want you to please pop in for tea again on Wednesday and I'm sure, in the meantime, I'll get to the bottom of this whole business.

WIFE: Oh, you are a dearie, you are.

COLONEL: Oh, I say . . . just one final point. What is your husband's first name, Mrs. Din?

WIFE: Oh. 'Is first name is "Gunga", love.

COLONEL: Gunga. Splendid! I'll take this right to the top. Now you be sure to write to Mr. Din and tell him everything's going to be all right! Yes . . . quite . . . good show . . . and do drop in for tea again.

REMEMBER THE GOOD OLD DAYS

After several occasions on which the Prime Minister's earthy tongue had bruised the fragile psyches of Quebec truck drivers and various members of Parliament, Opposition Leader Robert Stanfield stated that his style was an affront to the office of Prime Minister. Well, it's never to late to mend, as even Scrooge discovered.

The master bedroom at 24 Sussex Drive. Trudeau tosses fitfully in his sleep while a raging storm hurls wind and rain against his window.

[*Over the sound of thunder, three ponderous and reverberating knocks are heard.*]

TRUDEAU: Yes, who is it out there?

[*The heavy knocking is repeated.*]

Whoever that is pounding on my bedroom door, will you please identify yourself or I'll call the RCMP!

[*The door slowly opens.*]

GHOSTLY VOICE: Pierre . . . Elliott . . . Trudeau! ! !

TRUDEAU: Look, who are you? . . . what do you want?

VOICE: You! . . . who hold the highest office in the land . . . You! to whom destiny has bequeathed so much . . . You! to whom the people look for example . . . while there is still time . . . *Clean . . . up . . . your . . . mouth! ! ! !*

TRUDEAU: Look, it's very late and I would like to get some sleep before to-morrow's session . . . uh . . . why don't you go over to the Diefenbaker's. I understand they still have a lot of their Hallowe'en candy left over.

VOICE: Before this night is over . . . you will receive . . . three visitors. First . . . the ghost of Canada past . . . then, the ghost of Canada present . . . and finally . . . the ghost of Canada still to be.

[*Clanking chains are heard approaching.*]

VOICE: Behold now . . . the ghost of Canada past. Mark well . . . what he doth say . . . and learn . . . how those who came before you . . . strove to ennoble and enshrine . . . the exalted office . . . which you now desecrate!

SIR JOHN A (*weaving in*): "The Maple Leaf . . . our emblem dear. . . ." Where is this libertine who would debase the highest office in the land?

VOICE: Over here, Sir John!

SIR JOHN A (*stumbling past*): I vow I'll teach him a thing or two about moral ethics!

109

VOICE: Not that way, Sir John! !

SIR JOHN A: I beg your pardon?

VOICE: I say, not that way . . . that's the window!

[*Sound of shattering of glass*]

TRUDEAU (*bored by the whole bit*): Uh . . . did I understand you to say there are still two more of these to come?

VOICE: Forget it . . . he blew the whole thing . . . O Tempora . . . O Mores . . . O . . . fuddle-duddle! ! !

HOW SOPHISTICATED CAN YOU GET?

Though nothing has been heard since, the Canadian Medical Association did announce some time ago that it was launching an investigation into doctors' incomes. While the Association doesn't suspect fraud, it will look into such practices as "sophisticated billing" whereby a doctor enumerates every single service performed during an office call and charges for them separately, thus getting more than the office call rate.

THE SCENE:

A doctor's office. He sticks his head out of the door, peers into the waiting-room. There is no one there but the nurse.

DOCTOR: Well, Miss Thompson, looks like we have a little breathing spell. Let's just run over some of this paper work while we've got the chance.

NURSE: Right, doctor.

DOCTOR: O.K. This first one is . . . ah . . . Mrs. Dudley Robinson, 37 Walnut St. (*Sound of nurse typing*) For services rendered October 30th during office call and hereunder set forth. Um . . . crossing office floor to answer knock on door . . . uh, opening door for Mrs. Robinson . . . um . . . ushering same in and offering chair . . . uh . . . lighting cigaret for same . . . um . . . small talk regarding weather, nursing brassieres and Prime Minister's behaviour in House. Loan of office pen to same . . . out of pocket disbursement, $25 . . . Total fee . . . oh . . . $75.

NURSE: Excuse me, doctor. Mrs. Robinson wasn't a patient.

DOCTOR: Well what was she doing in my office taking up my time?

NURSE: Don't you remember? She was canvassing for the United Appeal.

DOCTOR: Oh, my goodness! Yes, you're right! Thanks for catching that, nurse. Could have been a little embarrassing. Uh . . . make that total fee, $25. There's no point in gouging . . . as long as I get my donation back.

NURSE: Doctor . . . you're just so darn off-hand!

DOCTOR: Well . . . man doesn't live by bread alone. (*Phone rings. He picks it up.*) Hello? . . . Yes, speaking . . . the what? . . . Oh, yes, yes, of course . . . that was the liver complaint. You feel $100 is just a little steep? May I ask you, sir, if you have any idea of just how much of my time was spent clearing up that liver complaint? . . . Well, just let me tell you! I stood for over fifteen minutes at the meat counter of one of your Loblaw's stores, Mr. Weinstein, before they decided to take that liver back and refund my money. I didn't even charge you for the time I wasted standing in line at the check-out counter. Really, if you laymen would only stop whining and complaining over these petty, picayune matters. . . .

THE FROG AND THE PRINCESS

I searched the papers in vain for the follow-up to a story which appeared early this year telling of a London taxi driver who planned to send a bill for $60 to Buckingham Palace. The amount was to cover damages to his taxi when he stopped at a pedestrian crossing and Princess Anne drove her new sports car into his rear end.

THE SCENE:

A little walk-up flat in Paddington. Alfie and the Mrs. are discussing, over a cup of tea, how one gains restitution from royalty.

ALFIE: Daphne, I think you're crackers! I don't like this idea of yours one bit. I wish you'd put it out of your 'ead. I just want to post a letter off askin' for enough money to 'ave me cab repaired. Nuffink more. I think this bleedin' scheme of yours is daft . . . I mean it's like something Lady Macbeth would come up wif.

DAPHNE: 'Old your tongue and drink your tea. Robert Browning used to say: "A bloke's ambition should exceed 'is grasp." Shakespeare used to say: "There is a tide in the affairs of men." Now with chaps like that eggin' me on, do you think I'm going to sit around 'ere listenin' to you? I tell you, Alfie, we're never going to get another tide like this one. You can spend the rest of your bleedin' days in this rotten little flat, but not me . . . not when I get a chance like this.

ALFIE: But it's not going to work, Daphne . . . it's too ruddy brazzeer.

DAPHNE: Oh, shut up and pass me that pen and paper. (*Clears her throat*) "Your most gracious majesty. It is with grievious pain that I take pen in 'and to write you this sad

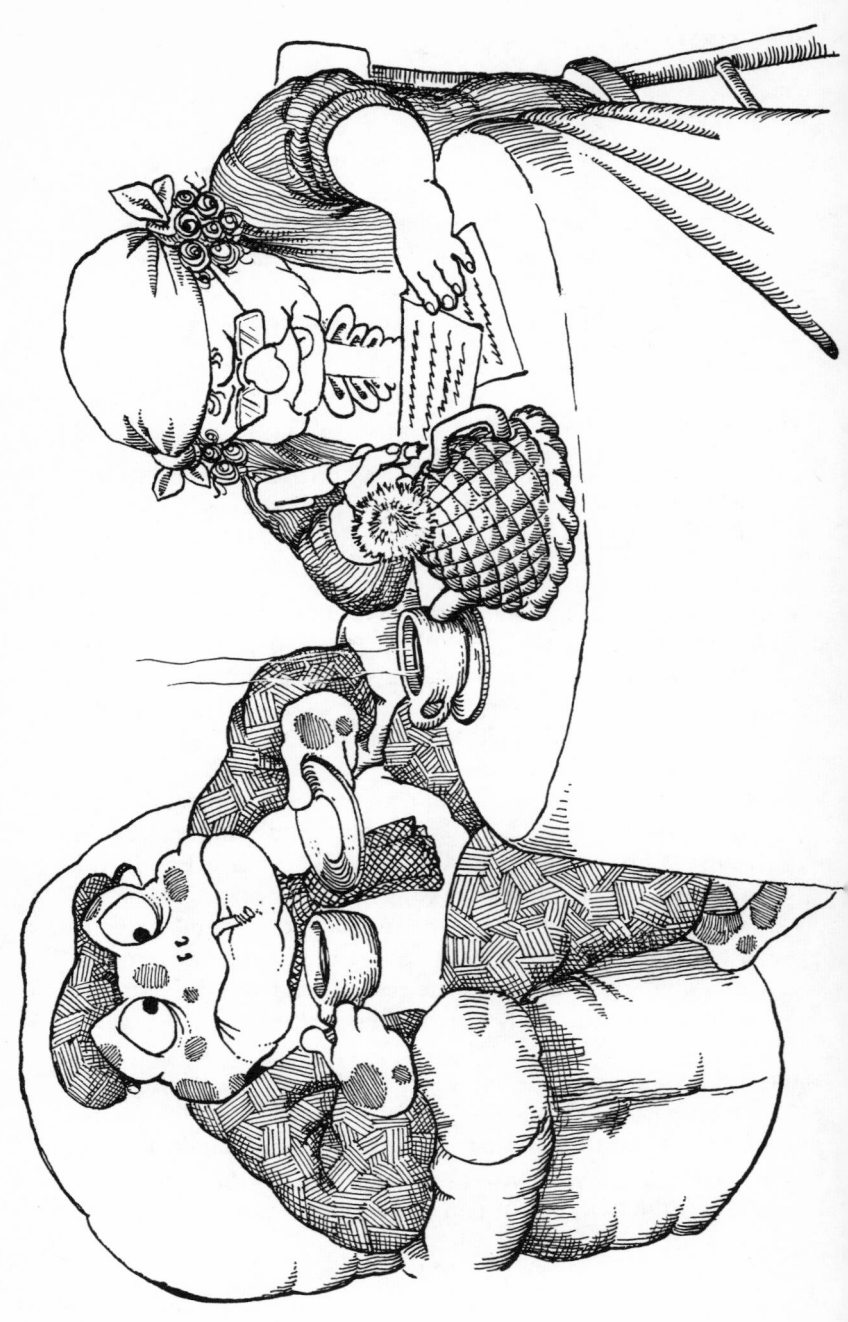

letter. As you may or may not know, my 'usband is descended from one of the oldest and noblest famblies in England.

ALFIE (*groaning*): Oh . . . lord!

DAPHNE: 'Owever, whilst 'e was still a babe in swaddling clothes, 'e was stole one day by some bad fairies wot was 'idin' in the bushes watchin', whilst 'e was swaddlin' on the front lawn of the fambly estate."

ALFIE: God 'elp you, Daphne!

DAPHNE: 'Old your tongue! . . . "They placed a evil curse on 'im, condemning 'im to a drab life of drivin' a bleedin' cab about the streets of London, until such time as 'e was kissed on the lips by a princess of royal blood, at which time 'is shabby clothes would turn into a suit of purple velvet and 'is old peaked cap would turn into a jewelled crown."

ALFIE: Come off it, Daph!

DAPHNE: "Last week, your young Anne went and put the kibosh on the whole thing when she ran 'er sports car up. . . ."

ALFIE: "Into", Daphne, for god's sake . . . "into"!

DAPHNE: "When she ran 'er sports car into 'is rear end and 'e turned into a great, ruddy frog."

ALFIE: Gor blimey! ! ! !

DAPHNE: ". . . with a big mouth! Now, I don't so much mind the damage to 'is cab, mum, but it is quite painful and traumatic 'avin to watch 'im sittin' about the place all day croakin' and catchin' flies with 'is tongue."

ALFIE: We'll both get five years in Wormwood Scrubbs for this.

DAPHNE: "Shut your face! . . . (not you, your majesty . . . 'im!) Normal conjugular relations are, of course, out of the question as I am terrible afraid of gettin' warts. 'Owever, mum, if you could see your way clear to send me a few thousand quid, I am quite certain that a Mediterranean 'oliday cruise would go a long way toward 'elpin' me to forget this whole terrible turn of events."

ALFIE: You are not mailin' that, Daphne!

DAPHNES I certainly am!

ALFIE: You are not!

DAPHNE: All right, Onassis, settle it your way. But if that young miss so much as runs 'er sports car over my foot I'll 'ave Buckingham Palace, Windsor Castle, Sandringham . . . the whole bleedin' lot! ! !

BACKLASH IN BRANTFORD

Police in Branfortd, Ontario, have been trying to make more than a hollow mockery of the old saying: "To err is human; to forgive divine." To improve their image with the citizens, they decided to designate one day a week as "Forgiveness Day." It would not be announced in advance but when it occurred, motorists who committed traffic offences on that particular day would receive a warning instead of a ticket.

THE SCENE:

Downtown Brantford. As traffic passes, CBC reporter Leslie Lovelace chats with the police chief.

LOVELACE: Sir, this magnanimous gesture of your police department . . . the practice of declaring a "Forgiveness Day" each week . . . has been in effect now for several weeks. How do you feel it's working out?

CHIEF: Mr. Lovelace, you're looking at a thoroughly resentful, disillusioned and embittered man.

LOVELACE: Sir?

CHIEF: A man in whose breast the milk of human kindness is lying in a rancid, curdled lump.

LOVELACE: What's the problem, sir?

CHIEF: We felt if we played the game, met the folks of this town half way, they'd reciprocate. And so, in all good faith, we decided to go with this idea of "Forgiveness Days." Well, by about six o'clock on the morning of these "Forgiveness Days" we were finding that the surprise element had gone . . . word had leaked out and spread around town that this was *the* day. Consequently, motorists were deciding to put all their eggs in one basket, so to speak, shoot the bundle, go for broke.

LOVELACE: Just how do you mean, sir?

CHIEF: They were driving their cars down the sidewalks, over the lawns . . . two guys parked their cars overnight in my office. And of course, the big fun game was right here at Branford's main intersection. Every car that came by had to drive over the foot of the cop directing traffic.

LOVELACE: Well, does this mean that you'll be abandoning the whole idea?

CHIEF: Oh, gosh, no! Of course. not! That would be petty, vindictive and the worst possible example of sour grapes. No, we just plan to modify the whole idea slightly.

LOVELACE: In what way, sir?

CHIEF: Well, we'll continue to pick one day a week at random, with no advance warning, but instead of calling it "Forgiveness Day," we're gonna call it Yom Kippur.

LOVELACE: Yom Kippur?

CHIEF: The day of atonement!

LOVELACE: What happens on that day?

CHIEF: Overparked . . . you get a year. Illegal left turn . . . two years. Running a red-light . . . three years and flogging. Then once a month we'll have Bastille Day. We'll just pick people up off the street for doin' nuthin! . . . put em away for a couple of years. We've also got a Dreyfus Day lined up each month. Anybody does anything that day, he gets kicked outta Brantford for life. We got another one in the works . . . Joan of Arc Day. Now this is really gonna be something . . . I think I like this one best of all. The way it works is . . . we get this big pile of wood set out on the main street here . . . all soaked in gasoline, see. . . .

PEACE IS HELL

According to President Nixon, when the Vietnam war ends it will be America's last war. "I seriously doubt that we will ever have another war," says Nixon. "This is probably the very last one." Unfortunately, he sounded more like a confirmed smoker than an oracle.

THE SCENE:

The Nixons' bedroom in the White House, in the small hours of the morning.

PAT: Dick, I declare. It's three o'clock in the morning. Why are you pacing up and down like that?

DICK: Pat, I'm sorry. I didn't mean to wake you up. I want to make that abundantly clear. I did *not* mean to wake you up.

PAT: Well, why don't you come back to bed, dear?

DICK: It's no use, Pat. I just can't sleep.

PAT: What's the matter, Dick?

DICK: I might as well level with you, Pat. Ever since we pulled out of Vietnam and swore that would be our last war, I've had these . . . well . . . I guess you could call them withdrawal symptoms. I get edgy . . . I bite my nails . . . I can't sleep. I don't know how to explain it to you, Pat. If you've never waged a war, you just can't appreciate how difficult it is to give them up.

PAT: But Dick, honey, it's such a silly habit. It's not only expensive but you know what medical science says. They now have conclusive proof that wars are injurious to health.

DICK: I know all that, Pat. That's the silly part of it. But every now and then, I start thinking about how good it felt when we had a war going . . . factories going at full production . . . lots of employment . . . people's minds distracted from domestic problems. And I just get that old urge to pick up the phone, call in my chiefs-of-staff, get the old war maps out and get one going again.

PAT: But, Dick! Now you know you don't really *need* a war. It's all in your mind.

DICK: No, Pat, you're wrong. It's not just in my mind. Now just let me say this. When you've been used to waging a war for so many years, it's a real shock to your system when you suddenly stop. Maybe we shouldn't have stopped completely . . . maybe we should have just cut down . . . fought smaller and smaller wars against smaller and smaller countries.

PAT: No, Dick, I think the only sure way is to cut them out completely. Look at the advantages . . . hundreds of thousands of people still alive who would have been dead.

DICK: That's a very narrow point of view, Pat. You're ignoring the other side of the coin. Since we gave up wars, I've been sneaking snacks out of that refrigerator every ten minutes. I've put on forty-five pounds. So you see . . . it's six of one and half a dozen of the other, Pat. No, honey, I'm afraid I can't hold out any longer. I'm going to call those chiefs-of-staff right now. We won't get a big one going . . . I promise you that . . . maybe just get into Northern Ireland or East Pakistan . . . someplace like that.

PAT: No, no, no . . . now you just wait. It would be a shame to get hooked again after all these years. Here . . . try this . . . it might be the answer. (*She opens a package of gum.*) Now you just pop that stick in your mouth, honey.

DICK (*chomping*): You know? . . . I think it's working! Pat. Let me just say this . . . you're a life-saver . . . in every sense of the word!

PAT: Starting to feel better?

DICK: Yep . . . it's doing the trick all right. That feels a lot better . . . not quite as good as a war, mind you . . . but I think it's going to help.

PAT: Now, you just come along to bed, honey.

THE BLUE MAX

It's been several months now since a Commons committee urged the federal government to increase the salary of the thorn in their flesh, the man who pounces on government waste and blunder, Auditor General Maxwell Henderson. The raise would be ironic, since only last fall they were trying to curtail his investigative powers and reduce his role to that of bookkeeper.

THE SCENE:

A chic cocktail party at 24 Sussex Drive, Ottawa.

DIPLOMAT: I must say, Mr. Trudeau, this is a thoroughly enjoyable party!

TRUDEAU: Oh . . . uh . . . thank you. So glad you could come.

DIPLOMAT: Everyone certainly seems to be enjoying himself.

TRUDEAU: Well, of course, the problem of trained help has always been a curtailing factor in this sort of thing but I do hope to be able to make 24 Sussex Drive much more of a fun place now.

DIPLOMAT: You will excuse me for talking shop at such a relaxed affair as this but I did want to let you know that you and your government acted most magnanimously in authorizing that $10,000 raise for the Auditor General. I mean, let's face it, he didn't seem to want to play the game with you chaps.

TRUDEAU: Well, I had a long chat with Mr. Henderson. We simply agreed to a straight forward deal. I offered him more money if he'd put more effort into civil service.

DIPLOMAT: And how are things working out?

TRUDEAU: Well, I would say that, all things considered, the arrangement seems to . . . Oh. Excuse me a moment, please. (*up*) Yes? What is it, Max?

HENDERSON (*sullenly*): Can I freshen your glass?

TRUDEAU: Oh, thank you . . . and, uh, Max? We seem to be getting a little low on canapes. Perhaps while you're out in the kitchen you could whip up another tray or two.

HENDERSON (*sighs*): Oh, all right.

TRUDEAU: Oh, and . . . uh . . . Max? Some of the guests will be wanting to drive home shortly and I noticed you only had about a hundred yards of the driveway shovelled. Could you get that finished?

HENDERSON (*exits muttering*): Blow, blow thou winter wind, thou art not so unkind as man's ingratitude.

TRUDEAU: Uh . . . yes . . . as I was saying, the arrangement seems to be working out rather nicely. He's not that much more *civil*, mind you, but we do seem to be getting a lot more *service* out of him. Yes, I think it's a good deal. We're very pleased with it. . . .

A MOUNTIE'S WORK IS NEVER DONE

Although most observers view the recent establishment of a Chinese embassy in Ottawa as a step toward better East-West relations, the RCMP are still sceptical. According to Commissioner W.L. Higgit, the move will mean more Red agents in Canada and, consequently, increased vigilance by the RCMP.

THE SCENE:

Inside the Chinese embassy. An aide is moving toward the front door to answer loud, authoritative knocking.

AIDE: "I wonder why I keep you waiting . . . Chow Mein . . . my Chow Mein . . ." (*door is opened.*) Yes?

HEAVYSET MAN: Hello, there! I'd like to welcome our Chinese brothers to Ottawa. I guess, when you move to a new country, it's all pretty confusing and upsetting . . . takes a while to learn the ropes and get the hang of things. That's why I felt you fellas might like to avail yourselves of the service I have to offer.

AIDE (*ignoring outstretched hand*): Please . . . what service you offer?

HEAVYSET MAN: Well, I operate a little Canadian hand laundry over on Metcalfe Street and maybe once or twice a week I could drop over and pick up your dirty shirts. I mean, you guys wouldn't have to stay in waiting for me . . . I could just let myself in, gather up any dirty laundry and have it back, all ironed and starched, in a couple of days.

AIDE: Please . . . all laundry done here by embassy staff.

HEAVYSET MAN: Well, yeah, but. . . .

[*Door is slammed in his face. More knocking Aide again opens door.*]

AIDE: You not hear me? I say all laundry . . . aaaaahhhh . . . yes, small boy . . . what is problem?

BOY (*looking strangely old for his years*): Mister . . . um . . . I was playing ball with . . . um . . . twelve of my uncles and we knocked the ball through one of your upstairs windows. Um . . . uh . . . my uncles want to know if it's all right for them to go up and get it?

AIDE: Very sorry . . . you tell uncles . . . ball now property of People's Republic of China.

BOY: Um . . . uh . . . well can I use your bathroom?

[*Door slammed. Immediate knocking. Aide opens door.*]

AIDE: No, no, no . . . impossible you use embassy bathroom . . .

CHARLADY: Oh, no, love! I don't want to use your bathroom. I was just wonderin' if I could come in one or two afternoons a week and do some cleanin' for you.

AIDE: No, please! Embassy have own cleaning staff. You go now!

CHARLADY: But, dearie, I need the money awful bad. . . . (*Horse whinnies from behind embassy shrubbery.*) You see, love, in me spare time I'm a member of the Canadian Equestrian Team . . . not to be confused with the Musical Ride, of course, and with the next Olympics coming up, I'm trying to raise enough money to get. . . .

[*Door is slammed. Immediate knocking. Aide opens door.*]

WITCH (*Rubbing hands and cackling*): I wonder if you or any of the other dwarfs would be good enough to tell Snow White there's an old friend of hers who'd like to see her.

AIDE: This Chinese embassy . . . no person here belong Snow White.

WITCH: Oh dear me, dear me. The mirror must have given me the wrong address. But while I'm here, perhaps I could just step in for a moment and show you my wares. I have lovely red apples. . . .

AIDE: No, no, no! You go now.

WITCH: . . . pretty combs for your hair. . . .

AIDE: No, no . . . you go now . . . please!

WITCH: . . . brightly coloured scarves . . . all kinds of pretty trinkets. Just let me in and I'll. . . .

[*Door slams.*]

AIDE (*retreating into embassy, shaking head*): Oh! What kind of country we come to . . . all same, hit real jackpot . . . spend all day answer door for Canadian ding-a-lings . . . no good . . . no good. . . .

THE NEW DEAL

Every food item sold in stores must now indicate, on the packaging, weight, contents and manufacturer's name . . . thanks to the efforts of Consumer Affairs Minister Ronald Basford. But you still can't get the answer to the most important question: "How much is it costing me per ounce?"

THE SCENE:

The sundries aisle of a large Canadian super market.

WALDO (*crumpling up a sheet out of his scribbler*): Well, that's another page wasted, Muriel.

MURIEL: Oh, Waldo! Did you make another goof?

WALDO: Well. it's been years since I done this here long division and messed around with them improper fractions. O.K. let's take 'er slow and start from the beginning. Now give me the Ron Basford rundown on that tube of toothpaste again.

MURIEL: All right . . . now the weight is three and thirty-one thirty-seconds of an ounce. And the price is $1.17.

WALDO: Got it. Now how about that other brand?

MURIEL: Can't seem to find the weight on that one:

WALDO: It'll be on there all right . . . Ron's put the fear o' God in all these manufacturin' fellas.

MURIEL: Oh yes . . . here we are. The weight is four and sixteen twenty-sevenths of an ounce and the price is $1.87 and three-quarter cents.

WALDO: All righty, here we go again.

MURIEL: You know, Waldo, even if we save a few pennies on each item this way, it's still costin' us 98¢ every other day for one of them giant scribblers. I think we're still gonna end up behind the eight ball in spite of Ron Basford.

WALDO: Oh, ye of little faith! Ron wouldn't have passed all them labellin' and packagin' laws if it wasn't gonna help us somehow.

[*The super market door bursts open.*]

COP: All right, you two . . . get your hands up! Now just what do you think you're up to in here at 2:30 in the morning?

BOTH: 2:30 in the mornin'!!!

COP: That's what I said!

MURIEL: Mercy, Waldo, we been in here comparin' prices since lunch time yesterday!

WALDO: Well, I declare! I never even noticed them closin' up shop.

COP: Well, the pair of ya just better come along with me. You'll get about thirty days for this!

MURIEL: Thirty days!

WALDO: There ya are, Muriel! How do ya like that for a savin'? Thirty days free groceries. Yessir, Ron Basford moves in mysterious ways his wonders to perform, but by golly he performs em!

COP: All right, move along now!

When Mitchell Sharp flew to Africa last March aboard a Canadian Armed Forces 707, the reporters who accompanied him were allowed to fly free. Yet whenever they accompany the Prime Minister on the same aircraft, they're required to pay their own way. No official explanation has been given.

THE SCENE:

The study, 24 Sussex Drive, Ottawa.

COLLISTER: Mr. Trudeau, I wonder if you'd care to answer for CBC National News a question which members of the press frequently ask but which, up until now, has remained unanswered.

TRUDEAU (*Stifling a yawn and glancing at his watch*): Fire away, Mr. Cannister.

COLLISTER: Well, sir, why is it that all of us can fly free when we accompany Mr. Sharp on a trip and yet we must pay our own way when we accompany you on the very same government aircraft?

TRUDEAU: Well, I should think the answer is quite obvious. Like everything else in life, you get exactly what you pay for. Although you fly free with Mr. Sharp, I'm told it's a rather dull trip. The press just sit there playing with their seat belts or sticking pencils in their ears. On my flights, there are little touches of gracious living . . . certain amenities and services which I feel more than justify the few hundred dollars which we ask you fellows to pay.

COLLISTER: Could you be more specific, sir?

TRUDEAU: Well, it starts right at the airport with our pre-boarding service. Reporters on crutches or in wheel-chairs are allowed on first. If they're under twelve, of course, they go for half fare. And since we believe that half the fun is getting there, we always serve tea, coffee or milk. On certain occasions, I might even fluff up a reporter's pillow. I'd also like to point out that there's a wide choice of in-flight movies available. We have Super 8 reels of me skin-diving, hitch-hiking in China or sliding down hotel banisters in London . . . all of which make the hours fly by. All in all, I don't really see what all the fuss is, about having to pay.

COLLISTER: Well, thank you sir, for clarifying the whole question.

TRUDEAU: It's been my pleasure, Mr. Chorister.

COLLISTER: And now, this is Ron. . . .

TRUDEAU: Incidentally, Margaret is now doing my bookkeeping. Would you just give her the $25 on the way out.

COLLISTER: The . . . the $25, sir?

TRUDEAU: Well, surely, you wouldn't think of coming into a lawyer or a doctor's home and taking up his time without paying for it. As Prime Minister I should think my time is at least as valuable.

COLLISTER: But sir . . . $25!

TRUDEAU: Well, if you want a $10 office call, buttonhole me sometime on Parliament Hill. But if you insist on making it a house call then pay the $25 and, for Heaven's sake, stop whining. I keep telling you, Mr. Cauliflower, you get what you pay for.

THEY ARE ONLY AWAY

The imminence of a narrowly averted strike in March, 1971, by news reporters against the CBC led me to ponder the disquieting question, if such familiar voices as Ron Collister, Norman DePoe and Charles Lynch were no longer heard interpreting the Ottawa scene, how would the CBC fill the void?

THE SCENE:

A CBC Ottawa TV studio where the program "Encounter" is due to start in ten seconds. Opposition Leader Robert Stanfield sits uneasily in the hot seat looking at the empty seats of his absent tormentors.

PRODUCER *(Over P.A. from control room)*: All right, quiet on the set everyone. We're on in ten seconds. Lighting! Get that boom shadow off Mr. Stanfield's head. O.K. Stand by! Ready . . . cue announcer!

ANNOUNCER *(Mellifluously)*: Good evening. From its Ottawa studios, the CBC presents . . . ENCOUNTER, another in our public affairs series in which well-known political figures face a panel of news experts. Tonight's guest is Mr. Robert Stanfield, leader of the Progressive Conservative party, who will be providing the answers to the hard-hitting questions of Charles Lynch, Ron Collister and Norman DePoe. The CBC sincerely regrets that our panelists will not be seen by TV viewers this evening. Because of a strike which their union has launched against the CBC, these men, at the moment, are over drinking beer in the beverage room of the Chateau Laurier Hotel where they have been since two o'clock this afternoon. Although they have steadfastly refused to be either seen or heard on any CBC programs, the three reporters have agreed, in the spirit of decency and fair play, to phone in their questions from the beverage room so that Mr. Stanfield, sitting alone here in our studio, will be able to answer them. Though viewers will not be able to hear these questions, they will certainly be able to see and hear Mr. Stanfield as he answers them. We sincerely hope and trust that this emergency arrangement will in no way impair your enjoyment of this hard-hitting program. And now, Mr. Stanfield, if you'll please pick up the studio phone I believe we're ready with the first question. [*Stanfield picks up the phone.*]

STANFIELD: Uh . . . hello? Uh . . . well . . . yes . . . but not too clearly . . . uh, is this Norm DePoe? . . . uh . . . well, you seem to be slurring a little, Norm . . . uh . . . well . . . no . . . I don't think it's on the line . . . uh . . . seems to be more in your voice, Norm. Uh . . . could I just have that question again . . . uh . . . seems to be quite a bit of noise over there . . . singing, glasses smashing . . . uh . . . no, it's not at this end, Norm . . . I'm pretty sure it's at your end . . . yes. Uh . . . well, that's a very good question, Norm . . . and . . . uh . . . just let me say this . . . uh . . . in answer to that one . . . uh, I'd really like to pop over and join you fellas . . . uh, but I promised Mary I'd come straight home after the program. Uh . . . hello? . . . who's that on there now? Is that Charles Lynch . . . seems to be so much singing and shouting . . . uh, yes, go ahead, Charles . . . uh-huh . . . uh-huh . . . Well, Charles, I think you already know my answer to that one . . . I've given it many times before but I'll repeat it again . . . uh, the answer is no. It seems to me if you fellas have run out of money . . . well, uh . . . it's time you all went home . . . well, now, there's no need to get foul-mouthed, Charles. If you needed the money for food . . . uh . . . I'd certainly lend it to you but . . . pardon? . . . Well, you just go ahead and phone the Prime Minister, fella . . . Who said that? Is that Ron Collister? Well, that's pretty rotten language, Ron . . . uh, put Charles Lynch back on . . . pardon? . . . he's passed out? . . . uh . . . well put Norman DePoe back on . . . he's what? . . . gone to the men's room . . . well, where's the waiter . . . uh . . . let me talk to the waiter, Ron . . . we still might be able to salvage this thing . . . no, no . . . no, I don't want to talk to you, Ron! . . . get off the phone . . . no, no . . . get the waiter . . . hello, who's this? . . . now just watch it, Norm . . . it wasn't *my* idea to get you back from the men's room . . . look, just get the waiter. . . .

HARK! HARK! THE LARK

Here's one for the cynics. Did you know that, every spring, all the lights in the upper floors of Toronto's largest building, the Toronto-Dominion Centre, are extinguished nightly for a two-month period to reduce the annual death-toll of migratory birds flying into the window-panes?

THE SCENE:

A darkened office on the top floor of the Toronto-Dominion Centre, in spring.

EXECUTIVE: Wanda, I must say I really appreciate your spirit of co-operation and company loyalty in staying late tonight to get these reports out of the way.

WANDA: Oh, that's all right, S.J.

EXECUTIVE: Well, I know the sacrifice you're making. I realize that most young girls your age would rather be out gallivanting around with fast young men . . . out there where the bright lights are . . . dancing, drinking and . . . God knows what.

WANDA: Speaking of bright lights, sir, would it be all right if I put the overhead back on? It's hard to see the keyboard with just one small candle.

EXECUTIVE: I'm sorry, Wanda . . . I guess I forgot to explain. You see, Wanda, this is the time of year when thousands of God's little winged creatures come flying back from the south and if I were to leave the lights on up here, well . . . I'd be signing their death warrants, Wanda.

WANDA: Golly, S.J., I've always thought of you as a hard-headed, driving business executive. I've never seen this side of you before . . . tenderness . . . sensitive concern for those weaker than yourself!

EXECUTIVE: Well, Wanda . . . as they say . . . God sees the little sparrow fall.

WANDA: I . . . uh . . . I was just wondering, S.J. . . . what's this liquor doing here on the desk?

EXECUTIVE: Well, Wanda, sometimes when birds strike their tiny heads against the glass, they aren't killed . . . just stunned . . . and as they lie there, helpless and alone, on the window-sill I try to force a tiny drop of liquor into their little, open beaks. It quite often revives them.

WANDA: But, S.J. . . . six quarts? Do that many hit the window?

EXECUTIVE: They come by in the thousands, Wanda. Even if one tiny life was lost because I skimped . . . well, I'd find that hard to live with, Wanda. Now, let's see. I left that box of wooden matches around here somewhere. . . .

WANDA: Wooden matches?

EXECUTIVE: Yes, Wanda, I make splints. Sometimes, just before the moment of impact against the glass, a little bird will seem to sense he's in trouble. Invariably, he'll stick his tiny legs out in a sort of skidding motion and, of course, this always results in a painful leg fracture. That's why I always keep matches on hand so I can place two splints along the injured leg and then wrap it up in some kind of silken material . . . uh . . . let's see . . . yes, this sort of thing will do nicely. . . .

[A loud ripping noise.]

WANDA: S.J.!!! My dress!!!

EXECUTIVE: I'm sorry, Wanda. Perhaps I misjudged you but somehow I felt that you were the type of decent, Christian girl who would gladly place the relief of suffering ahead of personal consideration or material things. I guess I was wrong.

WANDA (*Feeling just rotten*): Well . . . I . . . I guess . . . I mean . . . if it's going to help some little bird to fly again . . . I suppose. . . .

EXECUTIVE (*Fervently*): Oh, Wanda! On behalf of helpless little creatures everywhere who can't speak for themselves, I want to thank you. (*As the ornothological fervour mounts his arms enfold her.*) Wanda, you're so humane. . . .

WANDA: S.J.!

EXECUTIVE: . . . so ecologically concerned. . . .

WANDA: S.J.!!

EXECUTIVE: . . . so understanding. . . .

WANDA: S.J.!!!

EXECUTIVE: . . . so bewitching. . . .

WANDA: S.J.! ! ! !

EXECUTIVE: . . . so delectable . . . maddeningly desirable. . . .

[*A resounding glass crash as the entire window falls in.*]

EXECUTIVE: Aaaaaahhhhh! My head!

WANDA: S.J.! You're bleeding!

EXECUTIVE (*Gasping*): Yes . . . purple martin . . . came right through . . . caught me with his beak. . . .

WANDA: Golly, S.J., you better get to a doctor quick!

EXECUTIVE: Yes, I suppose so . . . damn nuisance. . . .

WANDA: Oh! S.J. . . . Look! Look!! The bird . . . it's still alive! Shall I give it some liquor?

EXECUTIVE (*Exiting enraged*): Don't you waste one drop of my liquor on that damn, clumsy, vermin-ridden idiot . . . hit it with a chair! . . . kick it out the window! . . . best laid plans of mice and men . . . damn, damn, damn. . . .

IT'S REALLY TWO MINTS IN ONE

When it isn't busy grinding out the country's coinage, the Royal Canadian Mint in Ottawa operates quite a lucrative sideline. It makes cuff-links — 21,000 sets last year — which retail at $3.50 a pair.

THE SCENE:

Ottawa. In the office of the Master of the Mint.

COLLISTER: I wonder if you could tell us, sir, just what made the Royal Canadian Mint decide to get into the jewellery business as a sideline?

MASTER OF MINT (*A little hurt*): Well, Ron, we don't really like that term "sideline." We like to think of this as sort of . . . well . . . cottage industry . . . because what we're trying to do here at the mint is not to make a little extra money on the side. We like to think that we're helping to alleviate the soul-destroying monotony of automated mass coin production. We want our workers to experience the self-fulfilling joy of creative work . . . the long forgotten pride of the artisan in his craft.

COLLISTER: Is the idea catching on with other crown corporations or government agencies?

MASTER OF MINT: Well, Ron, you know the old saying: "Monkey see . . . monkey do." Ha-ha. Yes, Ron, the cottage craft idea is really catching on. It's becoming the "in" thing with government departments and agencies. I just heard yesterday that John Munro is trying to get a Vic Tanny franchise for the federal Health Department. They also tell me that Fisheries Minister Jack Davis sells fish and chips wrapped up in Hansard to backbenchers right on the floor of the House. I'm just afraid that somebody's going to go too far and blow the lid right off . . . spoil it for the rest of us.

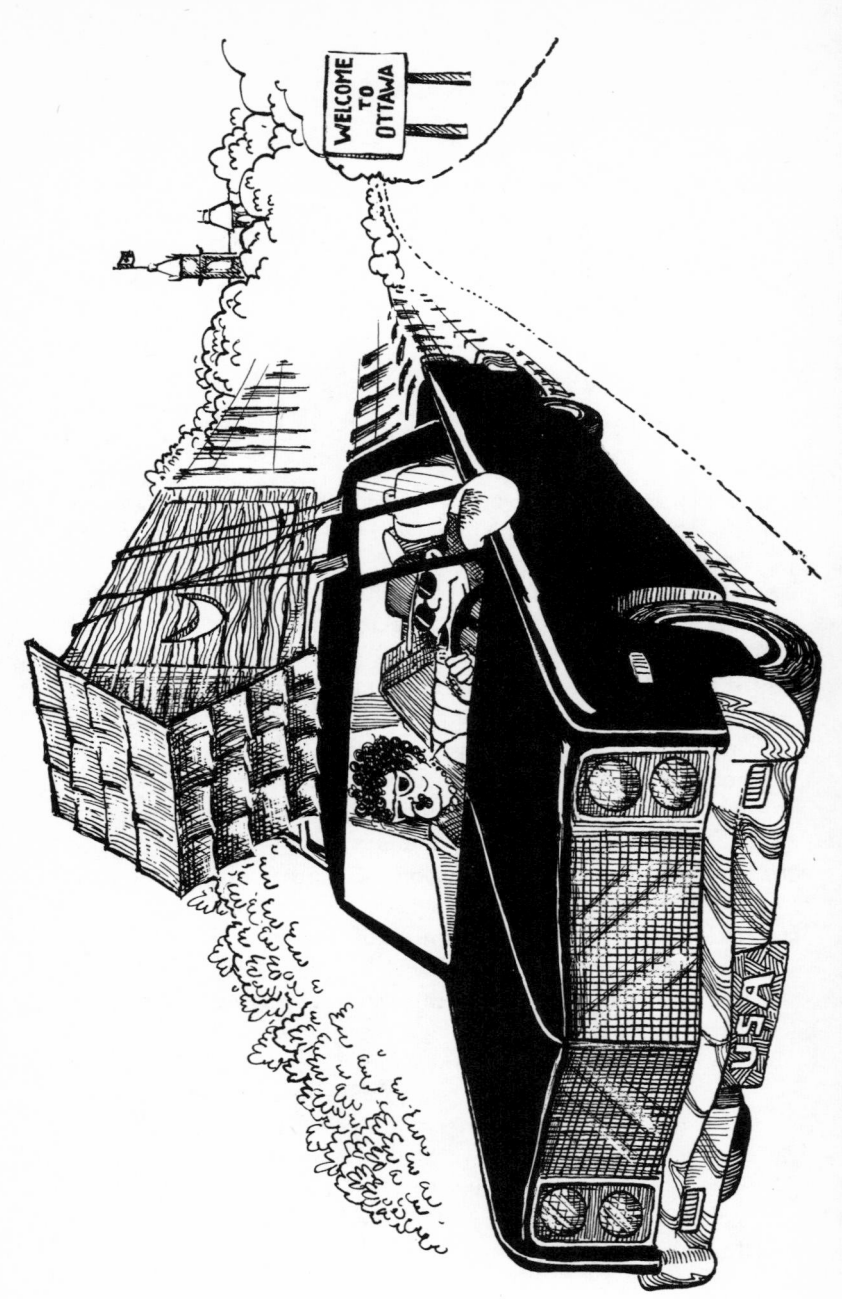

VOICE (*Fading on*): Ron! Ron Collister! Well, how the heck are you, fella?

COLLISTER: Oh . . . uh . . . hello there.

VOICE: Ron, you look like the kind of a fella who can recognize a bargain when he sees one. Now, Ron, I'm prepared to offer you a deal on an outhouse that you won't believe. These are hand-crafted units, Ron, made from the finest Canadian birch . . . non-rust hinges, a crescent moon cut into every door . . . your choice of two fast-selling models. The economical one-holer for individuals or the handy twelve-holer for Commons committees . . . ideal for those cottage weekends in the Gatineau Hills, Ron!

COLLISTER: Well . . . uh . . . not just at the moment . . . uh . . . perhaps. . . .

VOICE: Don't leave it too late, Ron, we're swamped with orders. . . .

COLLISTER: Yes . . . well . . . I'll . . . uh. . . .

VOICE (*Fading off*): Book early and avoid disappointment, Ron. They're really moving. I have an appointment with the Prime Minister in fifteen minutes. . . . .

COLLISTER (*To Master of Mint*): Who on earth is *that*?

MASTER OF MINT: *That's* the man who's going to spoil it for everybody!

COLLISTER: But, who *is* he?

MASTER OF MINT: There's one in every crowd . . . always somebody who has to overdo things.

COLLISTER: But, sir, *who* is it?

MASTER OF MINT: Oh . . . don't you know him? That's the president of the Privy Council.

Abdul Rahman is a royal medicine man living in Kuala Lumpur, capital of Malaysia. He was honoured by the Family Planning Board of Malaysia when they cited him as a symbol of planned parenthood and a shining example for all Malaysians. Although the 63-year-old Abdul has thirty-two wives, he has fathered only seven children.

THE SCENE:

Abdul's home in Kuala Lumpur where the BBC has set up its mobile radio equipment.

REPORTER: Good afternoon. This is Nigel Napier-Barclay of the BBC speaking from Kuala Lumpur, capital of Malaysia and home of this rather remarkable gentleman standing beside me at the moment. Mr. Rahman, you have thirty-two wives and only seven children. How do you account for this?

ABDUL: When the forces of darkness and evil attempt to lure my miserable thoughts into the physical world of wanton pleasures and false delights, I strive to withdraw at such moments into the much more satisfying and meaningful world of inner beauty and tranquility.

REPORTER: But surely, surrounded as you must be all day by thirty-two women, you must find this difficult to achieve. Just how do you go about it?

ABDUL: From the rising of each sun unto the setting thereof I sit motionless in the lotus position.

REPORTER: I see . . . the lotus position . . . that's where the left foot is placed on the right hip and the right foot is placed on the left hip?

ABDUL: Thees ees correct. And in thees position I strive for many hours to empty my mind of all worldly thoughts . . .

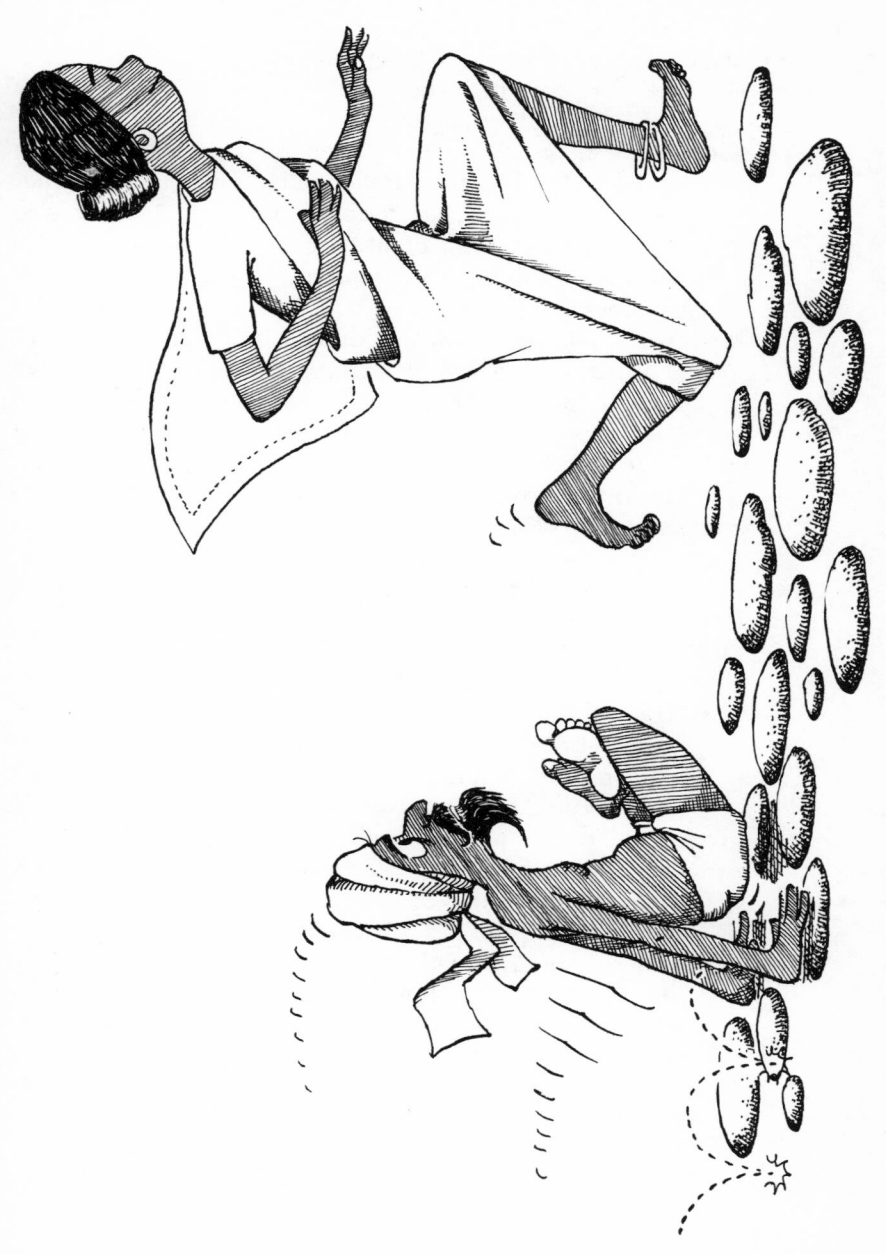

to let it turn inward through transcendental meditation and dwell serenely on the spiritual beauty to be found within us all.

REPORTER: I see. Then, of course, you emerge from this trance-like state spiritually regenerated and impervious to any of the physical appetites.

ABDUL: Oh, my goodness, no! No, no, no, no! I said I *strive* to do all this. The gift of transcendental meditation is not offered to all. As your people would say: "I jolly well cannot get the hang of it." I emerge from each trance much worse than when I entered it. All my wives look ten times more desirable.

REPORTER: Well, then, how do you manage . . . I mean. . . .

ABDUL: When you are my age and spend so many hours seated in the lotus position you do not snap out of it like that. (*He snaps fingers.*) I spend the entire night paddling around on my hands, with my contorted little body swinging to and fro between my arms. If I raise one arm to push open a bedroom door, I collapse and fall over onto my miserable face.

REPORTER: Well, thank you Mr. Rahman for taking the time to. . . .

ABDUL: I call out beseechingly to my wives to come and unravel my wretched legs but they laugh at me. . . .

REPORTER: Well, we certainly appreciate. . . .

ABDUL: Sometimes, they divide into teams and kick me about in the manner of a football while I cry out piteously to the Lord Krishna to put an end to this mockery. . . .

REPORTER: Yes . . . quite . . . well, thank you again for. . . .

ABDUL: Thrice blessed was Toulouse Lautrec compared to the torment I must endure nightly.

REPORTER: I see . . . this is . . . Nigel Napier-Barclay. . . .

ABDUL: The rosy fingers of dawn caressing the jasmine vines bring no relief . . . for though my legs have begun to straighten, it is then time to meditate again. . . .

REPORTER: . . . of the BBC. . . .

ABDUL: . . . and so, back into the lotus position again. This is the story of my wretched life . . . I don't know how I managed even seven children . . . it is a living Hell, I tell you. . . .

REPORTER: . . . reporting from Malaysia. . . .

ABDUL: . . . and if karma so guides your footsteps that you again encounter those mocking swine of the Family Planning Board, say unto them that I hope they all rot on a mound of jackal dung.

DOES HE OR DOESN'T HE?

The 1971 Canadian Census was still trying to get off the ground when it ran smack into the lowered horns of John Diefenbaker. Among the things Mr. Diefenbaker objected to was the implicit threat of a $500 fine for refusing to tell the government whether or not he had a flush toilet in his home.

THE SCENE:

Ron Collister reports to the nation from Parliament Hill.

COLLISTER: Not since the Gerda Munsinger affair has official Ottawa been so profoundly shaken as it has these past few days over what reporters are referring to as the John Diefenbaker Flush Toilet Crisis. At this moment, Mr. Diefenbaker is under house arrest and the government is still sitting after an all-night session trying to decide what to do with him. It all began three days ago when Mr. Diefenbaker chased a terrified census taker from his front doorstep, shouting angrily that the government had no business in the bathrooms of the nation. Subsequent phone calls by the Prime Minister to Mr. Diefenbaker brought the same angry refusal to divulge whether or not he has a flush toilet in his home. The Prime Minister then sought to ward off a direct confrontation and save his government the embarrassment of a showdown by placing an extension ladder against the side wall of Mr. Diefenbaker's home late yesterday afternoon and personally climbing to the second-story bathroom window. Mr. Diefenbaker, alerted by his wife, then ran out and pulled the ladder away. That evening, TV viewers across the nation gazed in shocked disbelief when the CBC interrupted its regular programing to show live coverage of Mr. Trudeau dangling by his finger tips from the bathroom window for forty-five minutes before being rescued by the Ottawa fire department. Mr. Diefenbaker has charged the Prime Minister as a Peeping Tom and he will appear in court next week. Meanwhile, according to late reports, Washington has entered the picture. An official note was handed to the Canadian ambassador two hours ago bitterly complaining that, although the White House contained seventy-five flush toilets, the President was able to use only two because of a severe water shortage. The note then went on to demand that the Canadian government reverse the course of the Mackenzie River, sending it south into the United States, so that the White House could again accommodate overnight guests. As the Canadian dollar continues to decline on the international exchange, Her Majesty the Queen has asked the Canadian people to remain calm and expressed the sincere hope that Mr. Diefenbaker will play the game and divulge the required information regarding, as she put it, his W.C. Meanwhile, Saskatchewan farmers have been pouring into Ottawa in a show of support for Mr. Diefenbaker. At last report, 476 outhouses had been dumped on the lawns of Parliament Hill and federal troops from Camp Borden have been placed on the alert. Throughout the day, as the crisis unfolds, the CBC will continue to interrupt its regular programing to bring you the latest developments.

COUNTRIES THAT PLAY TOGETHER STAY TOGETHER

The long, tense years of cold war between the U.S. and Red China, which saw the two giants eyeing each other in silent mistrust, may be coming to an end. The turning point was when Red China invited a U.S. ping-pong team to come to Peking. Thank God they weren't beaten too badly . . . A blow to American national pride at such a crucial juncture could have been disastrous.

THE SCENE:

A presidential press conference at the White House. While TV cameras roll, flash-bulbs pop and microphones are thrust at him from all angles, a distraught president tries to cope.

NIXON: Uh . . . gentlemen . . . please . . . uh . . . let me just try to handle one question at a time.
VOICE: Mr. President! Morley Safer . . . CBS News.
NIXON: Uh . . . yes, Mr. Safer.
SAFER: As of this moment, sir, where do we stand with Red China?
NIXON: Uh . . . well, let me say this. From the very outset, I felt it was a strategic blunder to send American ping-pong

players to Red China. I think it would have been quite enough to supply the ping-pong balls, the bats and the nets. But I think the actual players should have been air-lifted in from Formosa and given, of course, all the equipment and moral support America could muster. If this had been done, our country wouldn't be finding itself today on the short end of that 21-0 score.

VOICE: Mr. President . . . have you and your advisors had a chance to see a video-tape of that game?

NIXON: Uh . . . I have just come from the war room of the Pentagon where I have watched, for the past three hours, repeated screenings of that game with my chiefs-of-staff. It is our unanimous opinion . . . and I want to make this abundantly clear . . . that throughout the game, in open defiance of all the international rules of ping-pong, the Chinese players were using an illegal top-spin on all their serves. Now if we let them get away with this . . . if we don't make a firm stand now on behalf of all the small ping-pong playing countries of the world . . . well, I think they'll mistake this for weakness and try to get away with even more in future games. I think you'll find in maybe another year or two that these people will try to sneak in net balls on their serves . . . double bounces . . . rebounds off the ceiling, and God knows what. America does not want to stand idly by and see this happen to ping-pong. That is why, only ten minutes ago, as your commander-in-chief I issued an ultimatum to Red China through a neutral country, giving them twenty-four hours to strike that 21-0 game from the records . . . to declare it null and void before the whole world. Meanwhile, as a precaution, the second and fifth airborne divisions are being air-lifted to Hong Kong and all units of the Pacific Fleet are proceeding to battle stations in the China Sea. As a decent, Christian ping-pong player I pray to God these precautions won't be needed . . . but if all else fails we're prepared, at any cost, to defend the rights of ping-pong players throughout the world and uphold those basic rules we've come to love and cherish.

HEY! WHAT ABOUT OUR HAPPY MOTORING!

By the spring of 1971, England had just about had her fill of wrecked oil tankers spewing their loathsome cargoes onto her coast-line. The government announced in April that it would seize or sink any ship, even outside British territorial waters, which threatened to pollute the British coast.

THE SCENE:

Saturday night on the TV screens all across the nation.

[*The roar of a hockey crowd.*]

BILL HEWITT: Well, I'd have to say that one was a real cliff-hanger all the way, Ward! In spite of that courageous last-minute effort by Toronto, which saw them pull goalie Jacques Plante in favour of six attackers, they just weren't able to come up with the fifteen quick goals they needed to tie Boston and so the Bruins come out on top of a 15-0 score.

CORNELL: Right, Bill. Well, in just a few moments we'll be hearing from Foster Hewitt and our three star selection but first . . . this word from our sponsor.

ANNOUNCER (*Soft, earnest and compelling*): You know, friends, at Imperial it takes a lot of people with many different skills and talents to ensure that the gasoline which ends up in your car is the very finest. Yes, it's a pretty big family which stands behind that motto "Happy Motoring." One of the newest members is Dieter Von Luckner. Dieter, in our hockey intermission, we'd like to hear from you something of the perhaps small, but nevertheless important contribution you're making in the overall Imperial story.

DIETER: Jawohl! Vell, chust few veeks ago I join ze big family vas iss called Imperial. Maybe you are read in ze paper zat zees schweinhunds. . . .

ANNOUNCER: Schweinhunds?

DIETER: Ja . . . ze British. Zey are getting . . . how you say? . . . tight-up? . . . chust because few drops of oil out-leaks from ze tankers. Zees schweinhunds say zey vill sink ze oil tankers. Vell, I vas U-boat commander Vorld Var Two . . . so Imperial iss give me old job back.

ANNOUNCER: I . . . I'm afraid I don't quite follow. . . .

DIETER: Ja, ven ze schweinhund destroyer come near ze Imperial tanker iss mein job to . . . how you say . . . machen zie das silver fish . . . sssvvroooom!! . . . und sink zem!

ANNOUNCER: I'm sorry, Dieter . . . I . . . uh . . . I think there's been some sort of a mix-up here. I thought you were a night-watchman at one of our service stations.

DIETER: Nein, nein!! Have better job zan zat . . . make ze real contribute to get ze finest gasoline in ze car engines.

ANNOUNCER: Well, thank you and now I see Foster's standing by up in. . . .

DIETER: Ven ze schweinhunds come aboard ze Imperial tanker, ze tanker uber-leutnant he stall for time . . . how you say . . . create ze diversion. Maybe give ze schweinhund captain all kinds power player cards . . . froliche motoring maps . . . Zis give me time untervasser to pull down ze periscope . . . line up schweinhund ship in ze cross-hairs und zen . . . ssvvrooom! . . . ein silver fish!

ANNOUNCER: Well, this has been most . . . uh . . . interesting . . . but now. . . .

DIETER: Like you say . . . chust one of many people . . . very happy be part of Imperial family . . . iss great for be alive in ziz land of ours. . . .

ANNOUNCER: . . . I think we'll go to Foster Hewitt!

DIETER (*Singing*): Esso . . . Esso . . . uber alles . . . da da da da . . . da . . . da da.

GETTING TO KNOW YOU

Police recruits in Ontario are now getting a three-week course in psychology as part of their basic training. If you're going to get arrested . . . can you think of any place you'd rather be?

THE SCENE:

Mr. and Mrs. Average Citizen are speeding along Highway 401 headed for Toronto International Airport.

WIFE: Dwight, dear, at this rate we're not going to make the airport in time! The flight leaves in thirty minutes!

HUSBAND: Now look, Daphne, I'm already exceeding the speed limit. If we get stopped by the law you're never gonna make that. . . . (*A police siren closes in.*) Speak of the devil . . . that tears it!

WIFE: Oh . . . no! Be honest with him, dear . . . don't give him any argument. He might be a reasonable chap and we can get this over with fast!

CONSTABLE: Good afternoon, folks. Warm enough for ya?

HUSBAND: Look, constable . . , I haven't got a leg to stand on. I was doing 85 in a 70-mile zone. I'm truly sorry . . . now, could you write the whole thing out please?

CONSTABLE: Well sir . . . let me put it this way. I'm not so much interested in how fast you were going. I'd kinda like to get inside that mind of yours . . . browse around for a while . . . and see if I can find out *why* you were speeding.

HUSBAND: It's really very simple, constable. You see my wife has to catch. . . .

CONSTABLE: Uh . . . hold it just a second, sir . . . I noticed hypertension creeping in there . . . now just try to relax and keep your eyes fixed on this shiny badge as I move it slowly back and forth. . . .

HUSBAND: Constable, will you please let me. . . .

CONSTABLE: Ah . . . ah . . . ah! . . . Your eyelids are getting very heavy now . . . you're very drowsy . . . verrrrry drowsy . . . you're starting to sink into a deep sleep . . . that's it . . . your mind is roaming free now . . . back across the years . . . you're seeing yourself as a four-year-old boy . . . yes and there's mommy and daddy . . . three sisters . . . and a cute little brother. Now tell me, just how did you get along in this little family group.

HUSBAND: (*In a lisping piping voice*): I liked them all and had a real peachy time.

CONSTABLE: Great! Tremendous! That's all I wanted to hear! I kinda felt there wouldn't be any deep-rooted problems here at all. Sorry to hold you up, sir. Just remember to take it a little easy.

WIFE: Oh, thank you so much, constable! That's awfully decent of you. Dwight! Aren't you going to thank the constable?

HUSBAND (*still piping and lisping*): Fanks . . . oo tin pway wit my tiddy-tar if oo want to.

WIFE: Dwight, there just isn't time for fun and games. Now will you start this car and let's get going?

HUSBAND: I tan't weach de pedals, mommy . . . my foots is too short.

WIFE: Oh, good grief! Constable will you bring him out of this instantly!

CONSTABLE: Gee, lady, I'm sorry. We didn't get that far in psychology.

WIFE: But you can't leave him like this!

[*Husband starts to sing "On the Good Ship, Lollypop."*]

CONSTABLE: Look, lady, you can only cram so much into three weeks!

WIFE: This is outrageous. Bring him out of it this minute!

CONSTABLE: Lady, I'm sorry . . . I mean Freud and Jung spent a lifetime at this . . . I've only had three weeks . . . now will ya get off my back . . . boy oh boy . . . whenever the public wants a whipping boy, they sure know where to look. . . .

LITTLE RHYMES FOR OLD FOLKS

When it was announced in April of 1971 that federal MP's would be getting a fifty per cent hike in salary, senior citizens, barely getting by, must have raised an eyebrow. They'd always been told there just wasn't money available to provide decent pensions. Where was it all coming from now?

CHORUS:
Old Mother Hubbard, went to the cupboard
To get her poor dog a bone.

MOTHER H (*sounding like Trudeau*): Come on, old fellow. Hurry up.

DOG (*very old and feeble*): I . . . I'm . . . moving as fast as I can. When you . . . don't eat properly . . . it's kind of hard . . . to find the energy.

MOTHER H: Well, we're certainly going to change all that! Wait till you see the nice surprise I've got for you in the cupboard!

DOG: Surprise?

MOTHER H: Yes, I'm going to get you a nice juicy bone!

DOG: Oh, mercy! That sounds just wonderful! I haven't had a bone for so long, I've forgotten what they taste like.

MOTHER H: Yes, come to think of it, you do look a bit scrawny. Ribs sticking out . . . sunken staring eyes . . . dull coat . . . and your tail drooping dispiritedly between your legs. Well, we'll soon remedy all that. I'm going to open that cupboard and you're welcome to everything that's in there, because at your age you've certainly earned it!

CHORUS:
But when she got there . . . the cupboard was bare.
And so . . . the poor dog had none.

MOTHER H: Oh my goodness!

DOG: Is . . . is . . . something wrong?

MOTHER H: Well, that's certainly very strange! There doesn't seem to be a thing in this cupboard.

DOG: Oh, dear! I was really hoping there'd be some little thing I could munch on. That's . . . that's . . . disappointing.

MOTHER H: Well, I'm afraid there's really not much I can do. You can see the cupboard for yourself. Let's be rational about this. If there's nothing there . . . there's nothing there. The only thing I can suggest is that you go out and ferret through some of the garbage cans around the neighbourhood.

DOG: Well, if that's the best you can do, Mother Hubbard. . . .

MOTHER H: I'm afraid it is. My hands are tied. You can see the bare cupboard. If it's any comfort to you, we're both in the same boat.

[*She opens the door and the* DOG *goes out . . . crushed.*]

CHORUS:

Old Mother Hubbard . . . she sat down and blubbered
At the plight of that hungry old geezer.
But when friends came to dine . . . things turned out just fine
She'd forgotten to look . . . in the freezer! !

MOTHER H: All right, folks, don't crowd! There's plenty for everyone. Here's a beautiful piece of sirloin . . . a lovely filet . . . perhaps some of you would like this breast of pheasant? Eat up everyone, there's lots to go round! I just don't know why I didn't think of looking in the freezer earlier. After all, nobody keeps this kind of food in the cupboard anymore! !

THE GOODWILL AMBASSADORS

In April, 1971, 20,000 Chinese ping-pong fans in Peking's Capital Stadium gave a tremendous reception to a visiting Canadian ping-pong team. After such an auspicious start, surely Ottawa will follow up this diplomatic coup with other goodwill missions.

THE SCENE:

A government *Jet Star* has just landed at Ottawa airport, disgorging a solitary passenger . . . an RCMP inspector.

REPORTER: This is Leslie Lovelace of the CBC and with me is Inspector R.J. Monaghan of the RCMP who has just returned from Peking. Could you tell us, sir, the nature of your visit to Red China?

INSPECTOR: Under the auspices of external affairs and at the personal request of Mr. Mitchell Sharp, I took over the RCMP Musical Ride to perform at Capital Stadium in Peking.

REPORTER: Did the entire Musical Ride go along?

INSPECTOR: Yes, Mr. Sharp felt that we should care enough to send the very best. Under my supervision, we flew over sixty horses and riders plus, of course, our eighty-piece RCMP brass band.

REPORTER: This would have been quite a costly venture, then.

INSPECTOR: Well, as Mr. Sharp said in our special briefing before we left . . . when you're shopping for international understanding, goodwill and world peace you don't count the cost.

REPORTER: I understand you had quite a triumphal entry into Peking's Capital Stadium!

INSPECTOR: If I live to be a thousand, I'll never forget that moment! We rode in with the band playing "The World Is

Waiting for the Sunrise" . . . a great Canadian song as you well know. Canadian flags were flying from our lances and when that deafening cheer went up from 20,000 throats I could feel my heart pounding with pride.

REPORTER: It must have been a wonderful moment. Well, tell me, when did you first realize that the Chinese expected you to perform the ride on top of ping-pong tables?

INSPECTOR: That shock came about thirty seconds later when we suddenly noticed these twelve ping-pong tables bunched together in the centre of the stadium. I certainly don't want to sound racist but, you see, the only sport these yellow commies ever see performed is ping-pong. Naturally, they figure that anything connected with sport or spectacle has to be done on top of a table.

REPORTER: How did you handle the situation?

INSPECTOR: Well, we had no choice really. Mr. Sharp had drummed into us the fact that the future peace of the world rested on our decorum and good manners. So, after about two hours of heaving and shoving, we got all the horses up on the tables and, boy, you couldn't have slid a piece of tissue paper between em.

REPORTER: How did the Ride go?

INSPECTOR: Well the band struck up "The World Is Waiting for the Sunrise" and away we went. We lost a few horses off the outside table edges right off the bat but I still think we might have had a fighting chance if it hadn't been for the darn nets.

REPORTER: The ping-pong nets were still up on the tables?

INSPECTOR: Oh, yeah. Before we finished twenty bars every horse was down . . . we had to shoot about eighty-five per cent of the entire Ride.

REPORTER: What on earth did you do then?

INSPECTOR: Well the decision was pretty well unanimous. We figured we'd all go out, get bombed on rice wine and then make a collect, obscene phone call to Mitchell Sharp. But all of a sudden . . . as if on cue . . . the crowd starts booing and getting real nasty . . . shaking fists at us.

REPORTER: Goodness me . . . why?

INSPECTOR: Apparently some clown in the audience translated the title of our band music as "The World Is Waiting for the Rising Sun" and the rumour went through the crowd like wildfire that Canada was pushing for the resurgence of Japanese Imperial power in China. Anyways when they started pelting us with Mao Tse Tung books, some of our guys got a little chippy and fired a few warning shots. That's when the Donnybrook really started. I was the only one that got out. The rest of the guys are still in jail in Peking.

REPORTER: How would you say this has affected relations between Canada and China?

INSPECTOR: Oh, I'd say we set em back anywheres from fifty to one hundred years.

REPORTER: That much?

INSPECTOR: Oh yeah! And, incidentally, I'd just like to say to any Canadian going to China on holiday ... for God's sake don't take any flags or telltale insignia with you! Also, it might not be a bad idea to get a little plastic surgery done on the eyes, cause I think a Canadian would be lynched instantly over there now ... I mean, we really blew it ... you have no idea ... you just wouldn't believe the debacle ... I'm gonna have recurring nightmares for years over this one....

HONI SOIT QUI MAL Y PENSE

When the Trudeaus slipped away for their Caribbean holiday in April, 1971, Canadians were able to take their minds off the depressing unemployment problem and fly, in fancy, with the honeymooners to sunny Barbados and Tobago.

A New Brunswick farm kitchen. The husband reads his sports page while the wife rocks to and fro in front of the fire perusing the front page.

WIFE (*humming "Rock of Ages" as she reads*): Well, Alvin, I see here your favourite prime minister . . . the white hope of the Liberal party . . . is off soakin' up sunshine while the rest of us wallow in winter and unemployment.

HUSBAND: Now lookit, woman! Apart from the fact I got a hankerin' to read this sports page in peace, I've told you a thousand times this here's a democracy . . . you vote Conservative . . . I vote Liberal. But let's not bug each other. You've been ridin' me about that fella, Trudeau, long enough. I happen to like the man and I think he's entitled to a honeymoon.

WIFE: Hmmmph! I just wonder if Anthony Armstrong Jones would agree with you!

HUSBAND: Now what in tarnation do ya mean by *that*!

WIFE: Oh, come off it, Alvin! I read the papers same as you. Says right here on the front page, Trudeau's down there with Margaret!

HUSBAND: Yeah . . . she happens to be Trudeau's new wife.

WIFE: Are you sure? Coulda sworn he married some girl named Bernice.

HUSBAND: He married Margaret. Now will ya shut up!

WIFE (*humming and reading*): Merciful Heavens! Now that *is* sick!

HUSBAND: *What's* sick?

WIFE: Well, accordin' to the paper here, the pair of em are down there swimmin' in front of all them natives with no clothes on! Now that's gonna give Canada and white folks in general a dandy reputation isn't it! Skinny dippin'! Well, I declare!

HUSBAND: I think you'll find that's skin-divin . . . if ya look hard enough.

WIFE: Well, it's the same thing.

HUSBAND: No, it ain't! Skin divin', you wear a tight fittin' rubber suit.

WIFE: Well, that may be . . . but how do we know he keeps it on when he's under the water!

HUSBAND: Will ya hush up and let me read this sports page!

WIFE: Well, I guess the truth always hurts . . . don't it? (*the humming continues.*) Well, I never! Now if that don't beat all!

HUSBAND (*snapping*): What?

WIFE: Did you know Trudeau used drugs?

HUSBAND: Nope . . . I didn't!

WIFE: Says here he's been on barbituates for the past few days!

HUSBAND: Oh, my goll! That's *Barbados*, woman . . . it's an island.

WIFE: Well, it looks an awful lot like barbituates . . . the way they've got it wrote here.

HUSBAND: Well, it ain't . . . now will ya shut up?

WIFE (*back to humming*): Heavens preserve us! ! ! Now *that's* the last straw . . . it's bad enough havin' a Health Minister who smokes like a stove, but when you get a prime minister poisonin' the body God gave him with that filthy nicotine. . . .

HUSBAND: Trudeau don't smoke.

WIFE (*Exultantly*): Got you this time, Alvin! Read it and weep . . . says he's on tobacco right now!

HUSBAND: That's Tobago . . . she's another island.

WIFE: Oh, come on Alvin! Really! Them Liberals can brainwash you, but not me! I don't like the undertone of this whole smutty article . . . I'm just gonna phone the girls in the auxiliary . . . make sure they don't miss it! Yessir, Alvin, you can fool half the people half of the time but you can't. . . .

NO CAUSE FOR ALARM

Canada's Solicitor General, Jean Pierre Goyer, has publicly confirmed that the RCMP maintains secret dossiers on some members of parliament. Though pressured in the House by questions from John Diefenbaker, the Solicitor General has never given further details.

THE SCENE:

RCMP Headquarters in Ottawa. The phone rings and is answered by a clerk.

CLERK: RCMP Headquarters . . . secret files division. Oh, hello, sir! . . . He's what? On his way over! Well, yes, I read in the papers he was a little upset when he couldn't get any direct answers from the Solicitor General but I never dreamed he'd show up in person . . . Oh, no . . . no problem, sir! . . . no we can look after it, all right . . . but thanks for the warning, sir! (*Phone down. knock on door.*) Uh . . . come in! (*Door opens.*) Well, for Heaven sakes . . . come in Mr. Diefenbaker . . . this *is* a pleasant surprise.

DIEFENBAKER: Uh . . . you're looking at a man, sir, who's spent almost a lifetime . . . uh . . . fighting to preserve the sanctity and sovereignty of the Canadian parliamentary system . . . uh . . . a man who drafted the Canadian Bill of Rights . . . uh . . . a man who abhors secret files, dossiers and all the other trappings of a fascist state!

CLERK: Oh, my goodness, Mr. Diefenbaker! Please hold on. Now, first of all, let me explain one thing. These terms, "secret files" and "dossiers," with all the sinister connotations they evoke, belong in the mythical world of Hollywood B movies! Mom gets so darn upset when the papers use these hysterical terms!

DIEFENBAKER: Uh . . . excuse me . . . uh . . . did you say "mom"?

CLERK: Yes, I did sir. You see, since she was widowed, moms

tries to augment a rather meagre old age pension by keeping . . . well . . . sort of a scrapbook for us here . . . jotting down little odds and ends . . . human interest items she runs across. If you'll just step this way I know she'd be thrilled to meet you and I'm sure you'll find she has nothing to hide. (*He leads Diefenbaker to adjoining room, opens the door and calls.*) Moms! Oh, moms!

MOMS (*a very big woman in a calico dress which would be floor length except for the intrusion of a silver spur*): What is it, son?

CLERK: Momsy, this is Mr. John Diefenbaker . . . he'd like to see any little clippings or jottings on him that you might have.

MOMS: Oh, land sakes! Come in, Mr. Diefenbaker! You'll have to excuse this place . . . it's so untidy! I sort of play den mother to all our rooky constables . . . always makin' coffee for em in here . . . bakin' pies . . . knittin' buffalo coats and what have you. Now let me see . . . these drawers are such a mess. (*She starts rummaging through an old chest of drawers.*) I'm always meaning to file these things. Now let's see . . . what's this one . . . Louis Riel . . . hmmm . . . I guess we're finished with that one . . . Oh yes! Here we are . . . John Diefenbaker. Now let me just get my glasses and and wipe some of this flour off my hands . . . there . . . (*reading*) "John always turns up in the House with his finger nails clean and his hair combed. He is always eager to contribute to group discussions but doesn't take instructions too well. His attention span is fair but he has a tendency to fall asleep sometimes, especially during speeches from the Throne. If he will try harder to get along with others, I think this cheery, hard-working MP will be quite able to cope if he graduates next September and moves on to the Senate. (*Angry footsteps and door slam.*) Mr. Diefenbaker? Mercy, there's no need to go stompin' out in a huff like that. Can I get you a piece of apple pie?

CLERK: O.K. that's just great, corporal! You did it again! Thanks.

MOMS (*lighting cigar*): You're welcome. Any time these snoopers try to give ya a hard time, just send em in to me!

MINUTE WASH MEDICINE

The University of Miami has come up with an innovation which may well prove to be the solution to the U.S. doctor shortage. Starting in July, 1971, the university planned to graduate medical students at the end of eighteen months instead of the usual four years.

THE SCENE:

Lunch-time in the Medical School cafeteria of the University of Miami.

CHARLIE: D'uh, hi ya, Fred! Anybody sittin' here?

FRED: Naw . . . sit down Charlie. You had lunch?

CHARLIE: Yeah, but I'll have a coffee with ya.

FRED: Well, just think! Two more days and we'll be puttin' that old MD after our names!

CHARLIE: Geez, that's right! Ya know, I've never seen eighteen months go by so quick!

FRED: Ya goin' into general practice, Charlie, or do ya plan to specialize?

CHARLIE: Gonna specialize, Fred.

FRED: Me too. I figure those extra two weeks are well worth it.

CHARLIE: Decided on your specialty yet?

FRED: Well . . . I kinda like the sound of podiatry.

CHARLIE: You gotta be kiddin', Fred! There's no money in podiatry.

FRED: Whaddaya mean?

CHARLIE: Well, lookit . . . how many people do ya hear of havin' trouble with their podes?

FRED: Probably lots, Charlie . . . but they just don't talk about it.

CHARLIE: I kinda like cardiology, myself.

FRED: Not for me . . . geez, I can't even play Snap.

CHARLIE: Have ya given any thought to anaesthesiology?

FRED: Aw, that's a closed book, Charlie.

CHARLIE: How come?

FRED: I just happen to believe she was killed along with the rest of the Russian royal family. I mean, why flog a dead horse, Charlie?

CHARLIE: Well, I guess there's always radiology.

FRED: You're puttin' me on, Charlie!

CHARLIE: No, I'm not.

FRED: Radiology?

CHARLIE: Heck, why not?

FRED: You've only had eighteen-months training, kiddo. You're gonna be up against guys that have been in that field for years . . . Walter Cronkite . . . Marvin Miller . . . Lowell Thomas . . . Ted Husing . . . gee, fella, sometimes I wonder how many marbles you got. . . .

IF YOU CAN'T SAY SOMETHING NICE DON'T SAY ANYTHING AT ALL

On May 3, 1971, the Queen and Prince Philip began a ten-day visit to British Columbia. In a public message to all citizens on the eve of the visit, Premier W.A.C. Bennett requested that everyone "relax and let his hair down in a nice way."

THE SCENE:

The departures lounge at Vancouver's International Airport.

AIDE: Believe me, sir, I tried to reason with them but their minds are made up. They're going back to Ottawa on the next flight.

TRUDEAU: But this is ridiculous. I don't understand. They both phoned me from Ottawa just two days ago saying they were flying out to Vancouver and would be delighted to join me out here for the Royal Visit. I told them I thought it was an excellent idea to have more federal representation out here during the visit and they sounded quite happy on the phone.

AIDE: Well, they both seemed pretty miffed about something when I talked to them a few minutes ago.

TRUDEAU: Didn't they give any reason? It's just not logical to fly all the way out here from Ottawa and then turn around and head back on the very next flight.

AIDE: Well, they mumbled something about Premier Bennett and his public announcements . . . said he made it impossible for them to stay.

TRUDEAU: My goodness, all the man said was that he wanted everyone to let his hair down in a nice way.

AIDE: Well, that might have been it.

TRUDEAU: But surely they wouldn't be that sensitive!

AIR CANADA (*over P.A.*): Would passengers Benson and Basford, destined for Ottawa, kindly check with Air Canada information . . . passengers Benson and Basford. . . .

TO YOUTH FROM FAILING HANDS

Premier Bennett wasn't the only one making public announcements during the Royal Visit to British Columbia. The Prime Minister, in a Vancouver speech, got in a few licks at Canadian youth. He challenged all restless, unmotivated young people to go forth into Canada's far North and bring forth new cities from the wilderness.

A restless, unmotivated group of cabinet ministers stand sullenly listening to the Prime Minister, shifting uncomfortably from one foot to the other and not really knowing where to look, as he chides them for their shortcomings.

TRUDEAU: My goodness, it's easy enough to sit around on your back-sides doing nothing but shooting off your mouths, but if you want an incentive . . . if you want to put a little gumption where your mouth is, then just take a look at the scandalous situation in our far North. American oil and mining interests, armed with exploration rights and tax concessions, are disembowelling the land up there in a frantic, greedy scramble to send more quick dollars back into southern pockets . . . Decades ago, Russia recognized that her North was to be for human beings. That's why you'll now find cities of 100,000 in the Russian Arctic with high schools, universities, factories, farms and hospitals. While we've been whimpering about the insurmountable obstacle of permafrost, putting up a few bungalows on stilts, they've been erecting multi-storied apartment buildings and building giant hydro-electric complexes on that very same permafrost. While our native peoples live out hopeless lives in their miserable ghettos outside the white man's northern settlements, their counterparts in the Russian North . . . the Evenks, the Yakuts, the Chukchee . . . leave high school, enter the universities of Moscow and Leningrad on scholarship and then return to the North as engineers, farmers, painters, writers . . . to weave into the mosaic of national life the vital, robust strands of their own cultures. Our Canadian North, by comparison, is a travesty of indifference, shortsightedness and outright stupidity! Well, what do you people have to say to all that?

MITCHELL SHARP: Well, my goodness, Mr. Prime Minister, those are certainly strong words but why address them to all us cabinet ministers? After all, we just follow our leader. Why don't you play it safe and go after some other group?

TRUDEAU: Well ... uh ... have you any suggestions?

SHARP: How about all these kids coming out of high school and university?

TRUDEAU (*brightening*): Hmmmm. I must say the thought hadn't occurred to me. You mean ... Canada's youth?

SHARP: Well, of course. With a little luck, we might even get them to accept the blame for our far North. It certainly won't hurt to give it a try ... by challenging them, you see, it'll take some of the pressure off us here in Ottawa.

TRUDEAU: Hmmmm. I'll probably be meeting a lot of young people when I'm out in Vancouver during the Royal Visit ... perhaps I could fob off some of the responsibility ... good thinking, Mitch ... I'll certainly give it a try. ...

UPON THE QUEEN

In the spring of 1971 we learned that, like everyone else, the Queen was finding it difficult to make ends meet and had asked the British parliament to increase her annual income. However, unlike everyone else the Queen can't strike, work to rule or collectively bargain so if her requests for more money are turned down what can she do?

THE SCENE:

A modest, little flat in Paddington. The postman has just knocked and popped a letter into the hall. Alfie shuffles along in his slippers to retrieve it.

ALFIE (*singing*): Come, come, come and make eyes at me
Down at the old Bull and Bush.
Come, come, drink some port wine with. . . .
'Ello, 'ello, 'ello! Wot's this? (*shouting*) Primrose!

PRIMROSE (*approaching*): Wot's up, Alfie?

ALFIE: 'Ere! You remember that letter wot I wrote the Queen last month extendin' birthday greetings to 'er Welsh corgi?

PRIMROSE: Yes, luv.

ALFIE: Well, just look wot come in!

PRIMROSE: Lord luv us! It's from Buckin'am Palace, no less!

ALFIE: That there's the royal Coat of Arms on the envelope, that is!

PRIMROSE: Well, open it, Alf! 'Urry up . . . come on!

ALFIE: I can't, luv . . . I'm tremblin' like a bloomin' school girl.

PRIMROSE: Oh, give it 'ere . . . I'll read it. (*She opens the envelope, smooths out the letter and reads.*) "Dear Mr. 'Iggins. I wish to convey my thanks to you for the lovely greetings you so thoughtfully extended to my Welsh corgi on the occasion of 'is birthday."

ALFIE: God bless 'er!

PRIMROSE: "In return, I am pleased to be able to offer you a wonderful opportunity to better youself. Kindly append your name to the bottom of the list of names appearing below my signature."

ALFIE: Coo! There must be over 500 names down there!

PRIMROSE: Ssshh! "Then, send off five pounds to the person whose name appears at the top of the list."

ALFIE: Well, I mean . . . that's 'er own name there on top . . . that's the Queen!

PRIMROSE: Sssshh! "Next, send five copies of this letter to friends you can trust. It is most important that you do *not* cross out the top name . . . simply leave it sitting there."

ALFIE: 'Ere now! That's not quite right! That's not the way it's done. She's gonna end up wif all the swag!

PRIMROSE: Ssshh! "If and when your name should come to the top, you shall receive ever so much money. . . ."

ALFIE: Bloody fat chance I've got . . . I mean, er name's gonna sit there. . . .

PRIMROSE: Ssshhh! "This letter has been around the world several times. Do not, I command you, break the chain or you will have bad luck. Lord Nelson broke the chain and look what happened to him! Also, Joan of Arc, Christine Keeler, Jack the Ripper, (my this *is* strange, Alf) Mary Queen of Scots, Adolf Hitler. . . ."

WHEN YOUR LOVE WEARS GOLDEN EARRINGS

During the Trudeaus' Russian visit in May, 1971, Margaret, already a match for her husband in skiing and skin-diving, added an additional feather to her cap. She was told by the director of the Bolshoi Ballet that she'd make a good gypsy dancer and was invited to take lessons with the company.

THE SCENE:

Saturday afternoon and CBC's "World of Sport" is on the TV screens across the nation.

MCKEE (*over background of cheering thousands*): This is Tom McKee, slowly making my way through what has to be the largest crowd ever to attend a Grey Cup game . . . (Excuse me, would you let me through please) . . . I'm still about twenty feet from the Prime Minister but I hope to be able to talk with him in just a few seconds . . . (Pardon me, please) . . . Yes, Mr. Trudeau is directly in front of me now . . . standing just at the edge of the playing field, here at Toronto's CNE stadium . . . He's smiling . . . looking very pleased . . . and, indeed, well he may, because as those thunderous cheers attest, that has to be the finest opening kick-off in the history of the Grey Cup . . . (Can I get through, please?) Mr. Prime Minister! Sir! CBC's World of Sport!

TRUDEAU (*not even winded*): Oh, hello there.

MCKEE: Sir, you must be feeling very proud at this moment. They tell me that ball went at least sixty-five yards! How do you feel about it?

TRUDEAU: Well . . . it was a very good kick, indeed . . . there's no doubt about that . . . uh . . . but, in all fairness, I think I should point out that Margaret *did* have the wind at her back . . . Uh . . . last year, when they invited *me* to do this . . . and I certainly am not saying this in a spirit of resentment or sour grapes . . . but I *was* kicking into the wind. And the year before, of course, some stupid reporter got in the way . . . however, there's no point brooding over these things . . . uh . . . I've taken up gypsy dancing which I feel will strengthen my legs considerably and so, if they should decide to use me here at the Grey Cup next year . . . although . . . uh. . . .

MCKEE: Although . . . *what*, sir?

TRUDEAU: Well . . . uh . . . I don't want this to sound as though I'm putting a gun to their head . . . uh . . . but . . . I *have* been in touch with the Bolshoi people and . . . uh . . . well . . . peut-etre. . . .

ONCE BITTEN, TWICE SHY

While a new era of understanding seemed to be dawning throughout 1971 between China and the West, a sombre note of caution was sounded by former Prime Minister John Diefenbaker who felt the Chinese overtures of friendship might be nothing

*but propaganda. Said Mr. Diefenbaker: "I do not
trust Chinese promises!"*

The Chief's office on Parliament Hill where he is interviewed for CBC National News by Ron Collister.

COLLISTER: Mr. Diefenbaker, you've publicly expressed a rather cynical reluctance to accept the hand of friendship extended by Red China. You've further said that you do not trust Chinese promises. Could you tell us, sir, on what you base this comment?

DIEFENBAKER: Uh . . . Mr. Collister . . . uh . . . during the many years that I have served this country . . . uh . . . either as Prime Minister or as leader of the opposition . . . I have had . . . uh . . . copious occasions on which I have accepted with goodwill . . . uh . . . trust . . . uh, indeed, with excitement and high hopes . . . uh . . . promises made by the Chinese. In every single instance, I have seen my hopes and expectations . . . uh . . . vanish into nothingness as I waited in vain for those promises to be fulfilled.

COLLISTER: But sir . . . can you offer us anything specific . . . any concrete examples to back up this generalization . . . this blanket indictment.

DIEFENBAKER: Uh . . . Mr. Collister . . . uh . . . I'm quite used to you Doubting Thomases of the Fourth Estate. For this reason, I have brought along with me this irrefutable, documentary evidence which I have been saving for just such an occasion as this. You're at liberty to take any of these documents and read them at random. Uh . . . here . . . take this . . . go ahead . . . read it . . . read it.

COLLISTER: "A dark stranger will enter your life, changing it for the better."

DIEFENBAKER: Uh . . . I got that out of a fortune cookie the first time I met Dalton Camp and he took me out for Chinese food.

COLLISTER: "Great joy and peace of mind will be yours when

you discover the love that is in the hearts of those around you."

DIEFENBAKER: Hmmmph! The day after I dug that one out of my fortune cookie, the Liberals got hold of the Gerda Munsinger story!

COLLISTER: But surely, sir, you're not basing your remarks on. . . .

DIEFENBAKER: Uh . . . don't talk to me, sir, of Chinese promises! Oh, I don't mind the fortune cookies . . . uh . . . as a matter of fact they're rather tasty . . . but those promises inside aren't worth the paper they're printed on! They never come true . . . uh . . . all hogwash . . . uh . . . promises . . . promises . . . promises. . . .

FOLLOW ME — I'M RIGHT BEHIND YOU

An agreement signed by Prime Minister Trudeau and Premier Kosygin, during the former's visit to Russia in May, 1971, provides for a co-operative exchange between Canada and Russia of research skills and techniques which will enable both countries to develop fully the vast Arctic area which they share in common.

THE SCENE:

An office in the Kremlin jammed with dignitaries and members of the world press, there to cover the historic signing.

REPORTER (*shouting over the din of voices*): Gentlemen! Can we get a shot of you both with your pens just poised over the document? That's it . . . great! . . . hold it!

REPORTER: Can we have a statement from each of you! Mr. Kosygin!

KOSYGIN: Da Soviet Union velcome dees hexchange weeth good Harctic neighbour . . . Canada! To Meester Trudeau am wery pleased to offer all our research . . . hengineering . . . meteorological . . . hagricultural . . . all thees which make possible for us and will make possible for Canada to build great cities in Harctic, served by giant hydro-helectric projects . . . all thees made possible by skills and heducation of native peoples in hindustry and in farming.

TRUDEAU: Thank you, Mr. Kosygin. And, in return, I would like to offer to you all the experience which my country has had in Arctic development and which you will find here in this humble brochure.

KOSYGIN: Humble brochure?

TRUDEAU: Uh . . . yes. I also have two others for you . . . one from Gulf and one from Socony-Mobil. They give the names and addresses of company officers if you're interested in some quick rubles from royalties.

KOSYGIN: Ah . . . yes.

TRUDEAU: I'd also like to present to you this handsomely bound volume, containing the names of American sportsmen whom we've been inviting to come up and shoot our polar bears. The hunting licenses aren't all that lucrative but they tip well and it keeps the Eskimo guides and cooks going for a day or two.

KOSYGIN: Da . . . da . . . ees good to know!

TRUDEAU: Now, I realize that your people already know how to produce eggs, milk, butter, meat, vegetables and so on, in the Arctic . . . but . . . uh, well if you ever have a bad year you might find this rather helpful. Oh, perhaps I should mention that most of those prices will be a little higher now . . . uh . . . that price list was published by the Hudson Bay Company three years ago.

KOSYGIN (*stunned*): Ees wery, wery high!

TRUDEAU: Let's see, now . . . I think we're starting to reach the bottom of the old know-how barrel, here. Oh! Hold on. Here's a list of some Canadian department stores that can sell some of the industrial products of your native people for a small cut . . . you know, things like ookpik dolls . . . soapstone carvings and what have you.

KOSYGIN: Ees everything?

TRUDEAU: Well . . . uh . . . we can also let you have this copy of Madame Benoit's Arctic cook book . . . *Forty Wonderful Things You Can Do with Snow*. Now, let's just see what else we have in Santa's bag here . . . oh, here's a free membership in the Action Canada party . . . uh . . . oh! by the way, if you're interested, we'd also be prepared to throw in Mr. Chretien, our Minister of Northern Affairs . . . uh . . .

KOSYGIN: Nyet . . . nyet.

TRUDEAU: Well, I guess that just about does it, then. I certainly hope you'll be able to benefit from all this and do feel free to call on us . . . I really mean this . . . and ask us about any aspect of Arctic development that may be bothering you . . . we're always glad to help.

MY BNA LIES OVER THE OCEAN

Future historians will look back with pride on 1971, the year when we almost got our Canadian constitution back from the British government. Justice Minister John Turner even got as far as meeting in London with British government officials to discuss the procedure to be followed in bringing back the BNA Act for amendment—if we can ever agree on the amendments.

Down beneath the streets of old London in the crypt where the Parliament at Westminister keeps its old, historic documents.

TURNER (*with a hollow echo to his voice*): I hate to put you to all this trouble, sir.

ARCHIVIST: No trouble at all, Mr. Turner.

TURNER: I just felt that, while I'm over here talking to your government people about getting our Constitution back, it would be nice to have a look at the document itself.

ARCHIVIST: Oh yes . . . quite . . . quite . . . well, I'm sorry it's taking me so long to put my hands on it. I know we have that BNA document here somewhere, but you see, I'm just in the process of taking over from my father. He's been National Archivist for over seventy years and he's retiring next month at the age of ninety-seven. Hold on one moment . . . I'll call him over. I'm sure he'll know where it is. Father! . . . Father! !

FATHER (*in a thin quavering voice*): Coming, your majesty! (*He approaches shrivelled and bent . . . feet shuffling.*)

ARCHIVIST: No, no, father. It's only Albert.

FATHER: Prince . . . Albert? (*He attempts to genuflect.*)

ARCHIVIST: No, father . . . Albert . . . your son. This gentleman here has come all the way from Canada and he'd very much like to see the BNA Act.

FATHER: Oh . . . yes . . . of course . . . I think it's here somewhere . . . I remember seeing it the other day when Lloyd George was in here . . . yes . . . (*Faded parchments fly hither and yon as he ferrets through musty old drawers.*) Oh! Dear me . . . often wondered where that one got to . . . Magna Carta . . . would you settle for that? All the same, you know . . . legalistic gobbledy gook. . . .

TURNER: Well . . . I *would* like to see the original BNA Act, sir.

FATHER: May I ask what your interest in it might be, young man?

ARCHIVIST: Father, this gentleman is a well-known Canadian. He's involved in a project to put the Canadian Consitution in modern shape . . . to revitalize it.

FATHER: Oh, my word . . . yes, yes, yes . . . I . . . I've heard about you . . . you're . . . uh . . . you're . . . uh. . . .

TURNER: John Turner.

FATHER: . . . Lloyd Percival! yes, yes . . . indeed . . . quite. . . .

TURNER: No sir, that's not. . . .

FATHER: You . . . you've built some kind of physical fitness institute in Canada. . . .

TURNER: Sir, if you'll allow me to. . . .

FATHER: . . . high time, indeed . . . yes, I've seen something of your Canadian constitution, my boy . . . your flabby government people come over here from time to time, you know . . . I've watched them at social functions, you know . . . no constitution at all, Mr. Percival . . .

TURNER: Sir, you don't understand. . . .

FATHER: . . . three brandies and they're flat on their face. . . .

TURNER: Sir. . . .

FATHER: We should look after our constitutions . . . only given one body, you know . . . I've always looked after my constitution . . . that's why I'm so clear-headed now . . . used to be able to hang by my feet from Marble Arch . . . holding Bertrand Russell in my teeth, I tell you . . . I'd like to see some of your Canadians do that, Mr. Percival . . . however . . . you've got the right idea . . . keep at it . . . shoulder to the wheel. . . .

AN OUNCE OF PREVENTION

From time to time, the spectre of the exorbitant refit of HMCS Bonaventure *turns up to haunt the federal government. As late as the summer of 1971, a Commons public accounts committee announced that it was calling two cabinet ministers to explain what steps have been taken to prevent such a thing from happening again.*

THE SCENE:

The tense, no-nonsense atmosphere of a committee room on Parliament Hill. The chairman raps on his water glass for attention.

CHAIRMAN: All right, gentlemen, I'd like to get this inquiry wound up as quickly as possible. This whole question of the *Bonaventure* refit has been very embarrassing and, certainly, Canadian taxpayers were justifiably outraged to learn they had to cough up seventeen million dollars for a job that was supposed to cost eight million. Now it's been some time since Auditor General Maxwell Henderson diligently dug up the sorry facts. What we want to know now from these two ministers of the Crown is what steps they've taken to prevent this sort of embarrassment from happening again. Gentlemen?

MINISTER ONE: Well, Mr. Chairman, we've thought this problem out long and carefully and I think you'll agree that we've taken the right steps.

CHAIRMAN: Well, come on man . . . what steps did you take?

MINISTER ONE: The front steps of Maxwell Henderson's house!

MINISTER TWO: We took them at eight o'clock this morning!

MINISTER ONE: At nine A.M., Max came barrelling out of his front door to go to his office. . . .

MINISTER TWO: He went off that verandah like a rocket. . . .

MINISTER ONE: Landed on his back halfway down the front lawn. . . .

MINISTER TWO: Should be in hospital for at least a year. . . .

MINISTER ONE: And at least another year convalescing at home. . . .

MINISTER TWO: So, gentlemen, you've got at least two full years before he starts snooping again.

CHAIRMAN (*exploding*): It's not Henderson we're taking steps to stop!

MINISTER ONE: Pardon?

CHAIRMAN: It's what you guys did!!

MINISTER ONE (*shell shocked*): We thought you wanted us to stop Henderson.

CHAIRMAN: No! No! Stop this outrageous overspending!

MINISTER ONE (*to Minister Two*): Gee . . . I didn't get that impression, did you?

MINISTER TWO: Gosh, no! I thought it was Max we were after!

MINISTER ONE: Overspending! Boy, that's going to be a tough one!

MINISTER TWO: Yeah, that's really going to take some thought

MINISTER ONE: Look, gang, I'm sorry . . . we're gonna have to check back with you on that one. . . .

MINISTER ONE: Yeah . . . we're gonna need a couple of years . . . boy . . . overspending!

MINISTER TWO: We didn't know you were gonna throw a curve like that at us.

DON'T PUT YOUR DAUGHTER IN THAT SCHOOL, MRS. WORTHINGTON

Gordonstoun, the famed Spartan school for boys in Scotland which educated both Prince Philip and his son, Charles, is going co-educational. The austere school which stresses physical endurance and toughness says girls from the age of thirteen will be admitted in 1972.

THE SCENE:

A modest home in Aberdeen, Scotland. The husband has just entered the front door.

ELSPETH (*from kitchen*): Is that you now, Hamish.

HAMISH: Aye, it is. Is my supper ready, woman?

ELSPETH: It'll no be ready for a wee while but there's a letter there you can be reading while you wait. It's from wee Mary . . . just come in the noo.

HAMISH: And how's the lassie likin' her first week at Gordonstoun?

ELSPETH: Och, Hamish, it's no a bed of roses. The lass is up at four each morning and out across the moor for a twenty-mile run. Then back again and twice over the assault course before she gets her porridge. She says, though, she's enjoying the weight lifting and the rugger.

HAMISH: I hope they'll no turn her into a great strappin' brute. After all, she *is* a wee lass.

ELSPETH: Oh, she's doin' other things as well, ye ken. Says she loves the weavin'.

HAMISH: Aye, that's good.

ELSPETH: Having trouble with the bobbin though, she says.

HAMISH: A loom no has a bobbin, woman. She must be meanin' . . . shuttle.

ELSPETH: Och, it's no that kind of bobbin and weavin, Hamish. They're teachin' her boxing!

HAMISH: What's all this over here on the table?

ELSPETH: She sent home a parcel of laundry to be done. Poor wee thing, she hasna the time to get it done at the school. They have to march four miles in the middle o' the night to a cold stream and pound their drawers and things wi' rocks. Wee Mary says it conflicts wi' her caber-tossin' practice.

HAMISH: What in the name o' goodness is *this*, will ye tell me, woman?

ELSPETH: Get awa wi' ye, Hamish! Have ye no seen a ladies bra, before?

HAMISH: Aye, but I've no seen em wi' only one cup, before!

ELSPETH: Och, yes! I forgot to tell ye . . . the bairn's taken up archery. Says they've got a very good instructor at the school . . . a big lass from South America . . . doon aroon where that girt river flows through.

HAMISH: The Amazon ye mean?

ELSPETH: Aye, she's from around there. She's been showin' the girls how they can pull the bow back farther to get off a better shot, do ye ken?

HAMISH: Woman! You're no tryin' to tell me that. . . .

ELSPETH: Now bide your tongue, Hamish! There's no need to make a fuss. After all, in this day and age of planned parenthood our Mary's no likely to need more than one . . . and it's doin' wonders for her archery! They know what they're about at Gordonstoun! !

WE'RE ALRIGHT, JACK!

In May, 1971, a conference of the United Church of Canada, held in Toronto, was told by two of its ministers that church music, today, is "truly appalling" and should be infused with more rhythm, life and variety. I'm sure there must be some ministers who wouldn't agree with this growing trend to modernize and "get with it."

THE SCENE:

Four ministers sit in a CBC studio, uneasily facing their inquisitor, hard-hitting, no-nonsense, Jack Webster.

WEBSTER: This is Jack Webster! I've rounded up what I think is a pretty fair cross-section of ministers and I want to find out from you fellows . . . point blank and without any beating around the bush . . . whether you go along with this trend today of always adapting, revamping and, in general, keeping abreast of the times and in tune with the needs of the public. Now, don't try to con me . . . speak your minds and give it to me straight!

MINISTER ONE: We'll certainly do our best, Mr. Webster.

WEBSTER (*wagging his finger at them*): All right now. Tell me if you all agree with this. You chaps all work in a place that's pretty well enshrined or sanctified. I'm quite sure you all feel that you were called there by God and that you are doing God's bidding. Now then, would you say that your work is not too closely connected or even concerned with the everyday world outside? I mean, is that a fair assumption?

MINISTER TWO: Uh . . . well, yes . . . I think that's fair enough, Mr. Webster.

WEBSTER (*leaning closer for the kill*): Now then! Answer me this! Would you ministers, deep down in your hearts, really like to see this sequestered haven of yours thrown open to the winds of change? Would you really like to see all that's safe and traditional and comfortable threatened by new ideas, new trends, new techniques? The doors thrown open, if you will, and the musty air driven out by fresh new winds?

MINISTER ONE: Well . . . uh . . . no. I can't say that I would.

MINISTER TWO: No, I think the old ways are best.

MINISTER THREE: Things that were good enough for our fathers should be good enough for us!

MINISTER FOUR: I'm a bit wary of moving ahead too fast. I think there's a lot to be said for caution and the *status quo*!

WEBSTER: Thank you for your opinions, gentlemen, and for dropping by. This evening I've been chatting with a cross-section of four ministers. . . . Edgar Benson, Jean Chretien, Robert Andras and Mitchell Sharp. This is Jack Webster.

ASK A FOOLISH QUESTION

The winds of change have begun to blow through the short pants of the British scouting movement. In May, 1971, it was decided that the traditional short pants of Boy Scouts would, henceforth, be replaced by long trousers. In this headlong rush to modernize, would the Girl Guides keep abreast of the Scouts? Who better to find out than hard-hitting, no-nonsense reporter, Jack Webster!

THE SCENE:

The merry laughter of little English Brownies and the thick Scots accent of Jack Webster fill the air of the lovely Sussex countryside as Jack grills one of the camp's Brown Owls.

WEBSTER: This is Jack Webster reporting to the CBC from a great big Brownie camp in Sussex, England. In this hard-hitting, straight-from-the-shoulder interview, I'll be firing questions at this lady standing here who calls herself . . . Brown Owl.

BROWN OWL (*in a very soft and refined voice*): Hello, Mr. Webster and all our friends in Canada.

WEBSTER: Now let's get one thing straight from the very start, Brown Owl. I want direct answers. Don't try to con me, because I wasn't born yesterday!

BROWN OWL: Oh deah! Yes . . . yes, of course, Mr. Webster.

WEBSTER: Now, basically, I want to find out how the Guides compare to the Scouts. First of all . . . these names that we hear of in guiding . . . things like Brown Owl, Premarital Lark. . . .

BROWN OWL: Mr. Webster! ! I can assure you . . . there are *no* pre-marital larks in guiding! !

175

WEBSTER: All right . . . all right! Then we'll stick with Brown Owl. Now, do the Scouts have anything like this?

BROWN OWL: No, they have a nomenclature all their own.

WEBSTER: What about activities?

BROWN OWL: Well, the girls go to camp and earn badges. . . .

WEBSTER: Do Scouts do this sort of thing?

BROWN OWL: Oh yes. We also have our cookie day each year. . . .

WEBSTER: Do the Scouts have cookie days?

BROWN OWL: No . . . they sell apples. . . .

WEBSTER: Now then, let's move on to this strange business you call "flying up". . . .

BROWN OWL: Yes?

WEBSTER: Answer me this . . . can you look me straight in the eye and tell me it has nothing to do with smoking pot?

BROWN OWL: Oh, my goodness! "Flying up," Mr. Webster, is a charmingly moving little ceremony when a young girl bids farewell to the Brownies and "flies" or moves, if you will, up into the Guides. We have several "fly-ups" each year.

WEBSTER: And the Scouts . . . do they have their flies up?

[*Sound of a resounding smack across the mouth.*]

BROWN OWL: I certainly don't go about checking! Now then, sir, if you don't want a cup of scalding Bovril in the face you'd better push off . . . you rotten egg! ! !

NO ROOM AT THE HILL

The government's new Re-Organization Bill to speed up and streamline the machinery of governing has resulted in so many new bodies on Parliament Hill that a serious shortage of office space has resulted. When last heard from, the government was planning

to solve the problem by evicting 160 angry MP's
from the Hill and moving them to new quarters half
a mile away in the old Union Station building.

THE SCENE

Confederation Square . . . throbbing arterial pulse of downtown Ottawa.

COLLISTER: This is Ron Collister, reporting from Confederation Square. One day soon, past this very spot where I'm now standing, 160 angry and dejected MP's will be making their way as they say good-bye to their Centre Block offices on Parliament Hill and trudge the long half-mile to their new quarters in the old Union Station building. At my side is the Honourable John G. Diefenbaker . . . the old warrior . . . the constant burr under the government's saddle . . . the one man who never takes a thing like this lying down. Mr. Diefenbaker, could you tell us what dramatic protest or defiant action you're planning?

DIEFENBAKER: Uh . . . I have given this matter considerable thought, Ron, and it seems to me that such an egregious, monumental atrocity as this can best be judged by the individual conscience of each and every Canadian.

COLLISTER: Then, sir, you're not planning any open defiance of the government?

DIEFENBAKER: I discussed such a stratagem with Robert Stanfield. Together, in our mind's eye, we tried to visualize the unspeakable tragedy of that ruthless expulsion of the 160 MP's. The moving vans carting away office furniture . . . the MP's being herded into waiting taxis . . . the tearful farewells . . . families parted . . . sweethearts rent asunder . . . perhaps never to meet again . . . Some MP's, no doubt, preferring the fetid swamps of Louisiana to. . . .

COLLISTER: Sir, do you really think it will be all that bad?

DIEFENBAKER: Uh . . . hold it, Ron . . . uh . . . preferring the fetid swamps of Louisiana to the cheerless, soul-destroying bowels of the old Union Station. Uh . . . Bob Stanfield was all for rolling up his two office rugs, lashing them together at right angles and staggering off with them over his shoulder, pausing at intervals along that half mile walk to rest and perhaps accept drinks of water from the onlookers. Uh . . . but I ruled against it. "We'll go quietly, Bob," I said, "with no hysterectomies. . . ."

COLLISTER: Histrionics?

DIEFENBAKER: Uh . . . please, Ron . . . I'm telling the story.

COLLISTER: Sorry, sir!

DIEFENBAKER: "We'll go quietly, Bob," I said, "with no histrionics. We'll make no cheap grandstand play for public sympathy. The Liberal MP's can go whichever way they want. I, personally, will lead all evicted Conservative MP's, asking only that the government provide us with an accompanying escort of RCMP."

COLLISTER: So you'll march quietly and obediently to your new quarters.

DIEFENBAKER: Uh . . . yes, Ron . . . with only one small detour.

COLLISTER: And what will that be, sir?

DIEFENBAKER: I plan to lead my small band of Conservative MP's by a circuitous route which will entail crossing the Rideau Canal. I haven't yet figured this out in detail, of course, but I have no doubt that, at the proper command, the waters of the Rideau Canal will part to let us through. Then, as the escorting rearguard of RCMP attempt to follow us, I will command the waters of the Rideau Canal to come together, thereby drowning the entire Ottawa detachment of the RCMP. But apart from this small token gesture, Ron, I plan no further public protest.

COLLISTER: Well, thank you, Mr. Diefenbaker . . . This is Ron Collister. . . .

DIEFENBAKER: Uh . . . are you *sure* it's "histrionics"?

COLLISTER: . . . reporting from Ottawa.

L'ENVOI

On June 25, 1971, nine years of blood, sweat, tears and toil, nine years of creating daily looks at the news for CBC network radio, came to an end with the final show and the termination of my contract. Into familiar, old Studio R on that last occasion strode A.K. Forsythe, of the CBC, leading nervously three distinguished guests. They sat at my old table and spoke into my old microphone.

FORSYTHE: A jolly hello to all CBC listeners everywhere! This is A.K. Forsythe of the CBC. Today, the curtain falls on the final appearance of Max . . . uh . . . Ferguson and his daily looks at the news. We do hope that his frolicsome mirth and merry jesting may have brought a smile or two over the years. And, more important, we sincerely regret any embarrassment he may have brought to those public figures whose hands lie upon the helm of our Canadian ship of state. Because of the undignified manner in which these public figures often appeared in Ferguson's sketches . . . because of the shockingly disrespectful speech he often caused them to utter . . . the CBC, in the spirit of fair play and good sportsmanship, would now like to offer these much maligned gentlemen the final word, so that listeners who believe in playing the game may, at last, see the other side of the coin . . . Gentlemen?
(To the tune of "They Didn't Believe Me".)

TRUDEAU: And when we tell you
　　　　How maddening it was. . . .
DIEFENBAKER: Uh . . . you'll never believe us.
　　　　Uh . . . you'll never believe us.
STANFIELD: Our . . . our . . . our way of speech, he ridiculed,
　　　　we . . . uh . . . we only hope you were not fooled.
TRUDEAU: By Max Ferguson's mouth,
　　　　His rotten mouth. . . .

DIEFENBAKER: And...uh...when we tell you
And we're certainly going to tell you,
TRUDEAU: He's going to end this disrespectful sham.
STANFIELD: No more will he use us. . . .
DIEFENBAKER: Uh . . . Or dare to abuse us. . . .
ENSEMBLE (*con spirito*): Fer-GOOS-on's gone . . .
And we don't give . . . a . . . DAMN!!